ALASKA C.

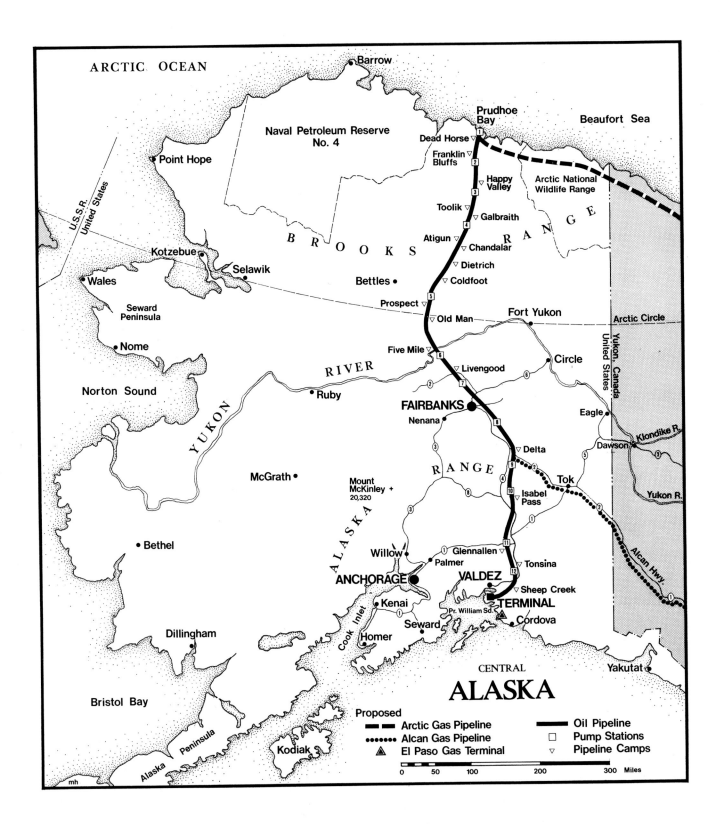

ARCTIC OCEAN

Barrow

Naval Petroleum Reserve
No. 4

Point Hope

Prudhoe
Bay

Beaufort Sea

Dead Horse

Franklin
Bluffs

Arctic National
Wildlife Range

Kotzebue

Selawik

Happy
Valley

Wales

Toolik
Galbraith

B R O O K S   R A N G E

Seward
Peninsula

Atigun
Chandalar

Dietrich

Bettles

Coldfoot

Nome

Prospect

Fort Yukon

Arctic Circle

Old Man

Yukon, Canada
United States

R I V E R

Five Mile

Livengood

Circle

Y U K O N

Ruby

FAIRBANKS

Eagle

Norton Sound

Nenana

Klondike R.

Dawson

McGrath

Delta

Mount
McKinley +
20,320

A L A S K A   R A N G E

Tok

Yukon R.

Isabel
Pass

Alcan Hwy.

Bethel

Willow

Glennallen

Palmer

Tonsina

ANCHORAGE

VALDEZ

Dillingham

Kenai

Sheep Creek

TERMINAL

Pr. William Sd.

Cordova

Cook Inlet

Seward

Homer

Bristol Bay

Yakutat

CENTRAL

Alaska
Peninsula

ALASKA

Kodiak

Proposed

━ ━ Arctic Gas Pipeline
●●●●● Alcan Gas Pipeline
▲ El Paso Gas Terminal

━━ Oil Pipeline
▫ Pump Stations
▽ Pipeline Camps

0   50   100   200   300 Miles

mh

U.S.S.R.
United States

ALASKA CRUDE

Visions of the Last Frontier

Photographs by Marcus Halevi

Text by Kenneth Andrasko

Little, Brown and Company 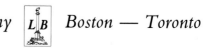 *Boston — Toronto*

First Edition

T 06/77

Library of Congress Cataloging in Publication Data

Andrasko, Kenneth.
  Alaska crude.

  1. Alaska — Description and travel — 1959. 2. Human ecology — Alaska. 3. Alaska
pipeline. 4. Alaska — Social conditions. I. Halevi, Marcus. II. Title.
F910.A69 917.98′04′5 77-4478
ISBN 0-316-33879-6

Designed by Janis Capone

*Published simultaneously in Canada
by Little, Brown & Company (Canada) Limited*

PRINTED IN THE UNITED STATES OF AMERICA

Preface

Within these pages are some stories and images of the people, the land, the paradoxes of Alaska in the throes of modernity. They are not meant to bound or fully describe the situation, as Alaska contains multitudes; please wander as you will. All the beautiful souls and all the stark raving mad mountains have coauthored this plea, and we are indebted to both.

The Pipeline saga may be the last chapter in the geographic history of the American frontier, hundreds of years of grinding quest for an elusive perfect place that has never been found. That has not cooled the impulse to escape and explore and walk free of the confines men and women devise for each other, as movement for its own sake has always been the central axis of the American spirit. The frontier has been declared closed before, but the events in Alaska are no postmortem; the expansion has not ended, but rather begun in a new form, undergone a metamorphosis that seats it even deeper within. Americans continue to ignore the past. We need a new vision of the trails left behind in order to chart a compassionate course ahead. Alaska is still in the early stages of bright boom, and is a kinetic remembrance of the way it must have been in the first colonies, the migration West, and the Gold Rush. Alaska has known too many booms already: the Russian occupation and decimation of the Native and mammal populations in the eighteenth century; the Gold Rush at the turn of the century; and World War II and the consequent development of Alaska for the military. It is time for the booms to end. Alaska is at once both an anachronism and a model for the future.

This version of the modern myth was made by two participants, present at the creation. Marcus Halevi visited the state in March 1975, photographed enough to sense the wealth of the situation, as well as its tragedies, and briefly returned East to spark the project and interest Richard McDonough at Little, Brown. Kenneth Andrasko led a mountaineering expedition to Alaska in 1973, decided the Pipeline would be worth studying, and returned for four months in 1974 to travel through the state and work as a Pipeline archaeologist in the Brooks Range, only to return again in the summer of '75 for more climbing and study. We met in September of that year in Fairbanks, as if by chance, while Marcus was finishing a four-month stint as a surveyor at the camp in Valdez. He had intended to be in town for only a few days before returning to Boston to finish the book, but after long discussions over beer and photographic contact sheets, we began to work together and generate a new conception of the book.

It began to evolve as an exploration of the final chapter in the documentation of the American frontier. Marcus was inspired by the tradition of the itinerant documentary photographers to whom we owe our image of the opening of the West, and the Alaskan Gold Rush: Timothy O'Sullivan, William Jackson, and Eric Hegg. Kenneth saw in Alaska the modernization of a Third World nation and sought to portray its rebirth, influenced by the work of several young writers investigating the relationship of people to the land that supports them: Frances Fitzgerald on Vietnam, Kenneth Brower, Suzanne Anderson. We discovered the inimitable Walker Evans and James Agee collaboration on the South's culture of poverty in the Depression, *Let Us Now Praise Famous Men,* and further developed a concept of parallel portraits of the idea of the frontier. These masters helped guide and inspire us while on our way.

As regular actors in the epic, we worked the grueling hours in the labor camps, boiled batteries in cabins at minus-fifty to get the truck rolling, flew around the Bush in choppers and planes, and sleezed in the saloons. As journalists we interviewed the appropriate actors in government, academia, and business, and anyone else with time to spare. We split up in December to return to the construction camps, Marcus as a surveyor again, this time at Pump Station 4 in the Brooks Range, and Kenneth in a staff position at Prudhoe. Spring brought a rendezvous back in Boston and time to unravel all the yarns and weave them together with a fresh batch of photographic images.

The two of us feel pleasantly indentured to a wide variety of gentle, insightful folks who contributed to this project in ways as richly varied as themselves. Kenneth tips his hat to Gordon Scott Harrison, for suggesting one rainy day in the mountains that journalism may be a more effective tool than academics for trying to make sense of the Pipeline; Jim Kowalsky and Pat Senner of the Fairbanks Environmental Center, for continual analysis, insight, perspective and a contagious sense of purpose, and to the people at the Alaska Center for the Environment in Anchorage; Henry Cole, Eric Forrer, and Bill Schneider for their openness, ideas and sense of Alaskan soul; Richard Fineberg and Craig Smith of the Fairbanks *News-Miner* for documenting and helping a newcomer understand the political complexities; and Terris Moore in Cambridge, for nurturing an initial interest in Alaska and always being available for invaluable historical background and criticism, though he is in no way responsible for the results.

Marcus would like to thank Bob Dreyer, Gary Minish, Stephen Wendover, Phil Johnson and Earl, for their cooperation in permitting a derelict Pipeline surveyor to occasionally disappear with his camera; Liz Kornblee, for helping seed the idea for the book; Yale Joel, Eugene Richards, and Ernst Haas, for their assistance, advice and criticism; Ad Beylund of Selawik, for patient assistance in an effort to understand the intricacies of the problems that confront the Native peoples; Renée Blahuta, for contributing a historical perspective of frontier photography; and Henry, Marilyn, and Janet for their friendly support.

A humble, deepest debt is owed to the people who actually appear in this book, under their own names and those contrived to protect them, and in photographic image. All of them are very special individuals who shared their sunsets, ambitions, and essential bond to the land with two curious wanderers.

At last, a round for everyone at the bar in honor of Richard McDonough, our editor, for his early advocacy and his ability to see the big picture more clearly than us, his faith and direction in the project, and his assistance to two newcomers to the art of making books. This particular one was created in the best Alaskan tradition, not by professed experts or scholars, but by two cheechakos learning fast but still new to the ways and wonders of the North.

The Pipeline signals the death of a splendid anarchy in Alaska, as a megalomaniacal pipe organ is being triumphantly assembled in the cathedral Alaskan wilderness to play one final funeral dirge. This book is a letter to the people of Alaska in a time of crisis, longing, and need, in the midst of an era of becoming, as they undergo a vision quest in the wilderness for what the future may bring.

"Indeed, one of the greatest pleasures of travelling was to find a genius hidden among weeds and bushes, a treasure lost in broken tiles, a mass of gold buried in clay, and when I did find such a person, I always kept a record with the hope that I might be able to show it to my friends."

— Matsuo Bashō
*The Narrow Road to the Deep North and
Other Travel Sketches*

K. J. A.
M. H.
Cambridge, October 1976

We were wanderers on a prehistoric earth, on an earth that wore the aspect of an unknown planet. We could have fancied ourselves the first of men taking possession of an accursed inheritance, to be subdued at the cost of profound anguish and of excessive toil. . . . We were cut off from the comprehension of our surroundings. . . . We could not understand because we were too far and could not remember because we were travelling in the night of first ages, of those ages that are gone, leaving hardly a sign — and no memories. . . .

Everything belonged to him. It made me hold my breath in expectation of hearing the wilderness burst into a prodigious peal of laughter that would shake the fixed stars in their places. Everything belonged to him — but that was a trifle. The thing was to know what he belonged to, how many powers of darkness claimed him for their own . . . utter solitude without a policeman — by way of silence — utter silence, where no warning voice of a kind neighbor can be heard whispering of public opinion? These little things make all the great difference. When they are gone you must fall back upon your own innate strength, upon your own capacity for faithfulness. Of course you may be too much of a fool to go wrong — too dull even to know you are being assaulted by the powers of darkness.

— Joseph Conrad,
Heart of Darkness

Every June the Salmon Run

Feel the hanging heat; see the ragged spruce and murky bogs come filtering through the twilight. Late in a summer night, yes very late. But still light now, it's always light in an Alaskan summer. Never the ease that night brings to the weary, always pushing on in a truck jammed in fourth gear. Starched cold out there much of the year, biting and bitter, but now it was fluid, and warm.

They pulled the dusty pickup to the two rusted gas pumps sitting idly in the center of a field of gravel ruts and stained, faded cardboard. One of the first dwellings of any sort since they finally straggled across the Yukon–Alaska border some forty miles back, an absolute barren land of scrub spruce and spongy tundra. Alaska at last!, source of richly interwoven dreams and fantasies, yet no jagged, violent mountains; no otherworldly herds trammeling the road, preventing passage. Just scraggly willow bush and bog.

There was no wind to blow away the dust the truck kicked up, so it hovered overhead and only gradually gave any indication of settling. A mangy collie crept out of a patch of milkweed to greet a boy of ten or twelve who appeared from within an aging Quonset garage nearby. The collie wagged; the boy waved and yelled something unintelligible before starting off for the main lodge.

A gentle elder, Elmer, in two pairs of canvas pants held up by scarlet suspenders wandered out to the pump, mumbled about dust and the price of gas to no one in particular, up to ninety-four cents a gallon here. No, nothing to do with the Energy Crisis, no, that was last year, according to the oil companies. Let's see, yah, spring of '73, just a year and a couple of months ago. No, there's always been a monopoly on life in the Bush ah guess you could say, yah, always been no other choice, never changed much. He blew his nose twice with the same rag he had used to check the oil and wipe the windshield, and wandered off.

"Yeah, well we got all the gas we need for a while," the pickup's driver replied to a young attendant, Randy, who had taken over. "That old guy Elmer couldn't do much with our sore hindends or lack of sleep, though." He measured and smoothed heavy duct tape over a fresh spiderweb crack in the windshield, and told of their excesses and shortcomings on the thousand miles of dirt road they'd memorized. Randy — well-curled cowboy boots, shirttails hanging out, flowing shocks of straw-blond hair — was an animated conversationalist, a bucking bronco ever telling stories with fingers and palms like a one-man puppet show.

"Well, hell, maybe Elaine can do something 'bout that!" Randy exclaimed, full grin. "We're really not open for business yet, seeing as me and my woman and brother Russell just got up here from Sand Point, Idaho, to run our own lodge, and Elmer, well old Elmer's moving pretty slow these days, he's getting on. But hell, come on in for some coffee 'fore ya head on up the road. Not much to look at around here anyway, not a damned thing for a hundred miles or so when the trees start to get a little bigger, but that's why nobody but us is around here. Hell! That's the whole point! C'mon in!"

The lodge was a lot like others along the Alaska Highway. Big game trophies that would make the Boone and Crockett Club record books, if anybody bothered to check, squinted from every dark corner of the comfortable main room. Several piles of *Alaska Magazine* and *Field and Stream* from the mid-1950's covered musty windowsills and overstuffed chairs shedding white cotton batting. A couple of hunting rifles, some gnarled and knobby pine, shamanistic carvings and watercolors the local Indian kids had done: the lodge was equal parts museum, pool hall, and Masonic Temple.

"Elaine, Elaine, how 'bout some coffee for these boys. Might as well see if that stuff's any good or not. Hell, I've been drinking it so long myself it don't even taste anymore." Randy fiddled with a Buck folding knife, then disappeared. Came back with a Remington 721 with scope, obviously for sale from the way he casually cradled it and fondled the bolt action.

"There been lots of traffic for you?" the driver wondered. There were two guns in the pickup already.

"Oh, picking up. Been lots of people through here, but always that way in June, I guess. Seems like there's plenty of people all set to get work on that oil project and talking of all kinds of big money, man! That's got to be talk, I mean big money! But ah don't know, hell — right here's as good as any other place. Besides, we only been here two weeks now. Elaine! more coffee for these boys, can't you see their cups sitting there empty? That stuff's not even any good, either, why . . ."

"Aw, you thought it was just all right this morning," Elaine retorted, pouring coffee. "Now you're complaining for the company, when I've got plenty to do around besides make coffee for you, why clean out all those rooms in the cabins and . . ."

"That's right, all that stuff. Like maybe some flapjacks for these boys . . . naw, don't worry about it, you guys, we're really not open yet, oh maybe another week or two. . . . So yah didn't get caught smuggling nothing at the border, eh? Those state troopers and customs folks are good 'en razor sharp, they impounded the dozen or so vehicles you saw sitting off to the side. Yeah, they get quite a few, they do okay. People are always bringing drugs and stuff across, like the old man — musta been sixty! gray hair and all — last week, got nailed with a shoebox full of cocaine just sitting on the floor in the back; they didn't notice till right at the end; almost got through. An' last year about this time, there was that shoot-out on the Yukon between about five guys on a riverboat and ten troopers from both sides. Two or three smugglers got killed and a couple of troopers, and two smugglers got away, a hell of a fight. Never too dull around here.

"But shit, no need to bother with that stuff now. Just get yourself a Pipe job up on the North Slope, hell any fool can do it. Lots of Indians up there making a couple of grand a week, and good food and don't have to work or do a damned thing, 'swhat I hear about it, not a damn thing. Plenty of jobs, eight hundred miles of pipe from Japan they've got stacked up in Valdez! Sounds like a big party; everybody'll be living fat for a long time. Might go myself maybe, dunno. Ohh, maybe after getting set up here and working on the place a bit, get the dog team started, that's quite a project training and feeding all of them critters, you know, got five already, and Muktuk's about to have . . . yeah, so might even do it myself, but hell, it's pretty nice here. And shit, I've never been past Tok Junction yet, ain't had a reason to . . ."

Raining again. Nothing unusual for Valdez, same old thing, but a bit of a bother nonetheless. That's Valdez, a gigantic stoneware urn, where the Chugach Mountains hurl their dying glaciers to the sea.

Lanky George Perkins led the way upstream. The chromium water surged to the rolled-down tops of his fisherman's boots, so he and Al stopped in midstream for a moment to pull the waders up to their full extension. The snows from some six thousand feet above Port Valdez harbor were swelling the streams still, in late June. The first day of the salmon run.

Humpies, or pink salmon, huge multifoot sea monsters rippling the surface on their way up the falls to spawn in alpine pools high above, thumped into the marine biologist and his tourboat-pilot friend. A humpback flashed furiously against the raging stream of beaten-gold light. There, another, a larger one, powerful tail and dorsal fin guiding it adroitly. The meltwater stream, despite its froth and the rapids' zinc-plated light in the fog and rain, was barely able to contain the fish. Their cameo-pink necks and bodies were flushed with exhaustion at the task of fighting ferociously upstream, a whole school of frustrated alpinists boiling in the quiet pools where the current doesn't go, feeding and awaiting the return of strength to renew the ascent.

It must be peculiar, George mused, for the humpies to go from life in the vast, uniform oceans to the specific tranquility and cruelty of the cool alpine streams bound in stone. Each salmon set out to return to the very pond of its adolescence, forgetting whatever it had learned among the ocean's schools of feeding fish out beyond. It's amazing, this aeons old mass rush to the mountains. Do they have any idea why they're killing themselves for this journey?

Starting to clear a bit, so George pulled off his heavy canvas hood. He pointed to the cannery apparatus in ruins all about, and exchanged stories of the Day family with Al. The family had built the salmon cannery and a nearby lumber operation just up a ways from Dayville Flats, both now defunct but still busy rotting. Every-

thing in Alaska is always busy dying, as soon as it's neglected; the land is harsh and jealous. Nothing is ever torn down or tidied up in Alaska, as if every hint of man's presence in the delicate yet savage land needs to be preserved to assist him in his struggle.

The mill had been powered by an electric generator built low on this same stream, Solomon Gulch Creek they had called it, and surplus wattage was sold to the townsfolk of the fishing village of Valdez on the north side of the inlet. Alfred B. Iles built the lower hydro-plant, and then another one higher up the creek in 1912. They powered the Midas copper mine at the top of Solomon Gulch, where the pools that fed the creek lay. An aerial tramway had brought down ore; the cables, pipes and towers of that airborne enterprise were scattered on the slopes. Innumerable tons of salmon were cut and canned here in years past; piles of galvanized tins still stood waiting.

But now, the flood of ripened pink salmon swam on by the cannery, streaked the stream's surface and occasionally crashed into the two startled waders, a thrashing horde of fish in heat. The grotesque humpbacks were launching themselves at the foamiest sections of the creek, the rapids over hidden rocks, vying for the darker, slower eddies just above. Each pool held gasping, starved humpies, some floating on their sides in exhaustion, scarcely a movement or more, all expending all the protein in their flesh to make the final trip home.

Al was just ahead when George yelled a warning: there was a grizzly bear mama on shore, *Ursus horibilis,* feasting on fresh salmon. They prudently retreated, and later continued until a Sitka spruce twig dropped in the stream to Al's left. In the tree above were two grizzly cubs, one higher than the other and on the opposite side; the spruce suddenly looked like the Tlingit Indian totem poles traditionally carved not too far south. To a flurry of growls from the returning mother, the two men hastily withdrew for the day.

The following morning George went to look at his

Two sourdoughs, Anchorage

Ladies in Valdez

sample plots on the tidewater mudflats. He was conducting a research project for the National Marine Fisheries Service near the bay on the long-term effects of oil on marine life in Port Valdez. The bay was once the site of the hamlet of "Dayville," and was now being transformed into the huge Pipeline Terminal tank farm and supertanker loading facility, the vast computerized wizardry that will command the entire operation by remote control. All of it, all eight hundred miles of forty-eight-inch Japanese steel pipe, 1.2 million barrels of high-grade crude a day over three mountain ranges and scores of rivers to the waiting fleet of 200,000 ton Very Large Crude Carriers, as these ships are known, in Port Valdez harbor.

Now, George was busy counting "these tiny thumbnail-sized clams called *Macoma inconspicua*. They're a field biologist's nightmare seeing as they're so damned small, but a statistician's dream, because of their very uniform distribution in this mudflat area." The field assistants use random numbers tables to locate a ten-by-ten centimeter square and carefully collect samples with wire screens. After their density and distribution are carefully calculated, some 360 *inconspicua* samples a year are sent to the lab in Juneau to sit there, possibly to be tested and further studied if enough time and money eventually turn up. At the moment, there is only enough of each to simply collect the basic data and samples and let them accumulate.

The purpose of the study is to provide comprehensive baseline data on what the mudflat is like in its pristine, natural state. The clam is a good index species for this work, and its reaction to various shifts in the tidal area's microenvironment can be noted over time as the terminal site development and operation proceed over the years. Unfortunately, the service had shifted its personnel to more important tasks, such as collecting data on the outer Continental Shelf in preparation for a series of oil leasing sales being conducted by the federal Department of Interior. So the field responsibilities in the study had reverted to the Pipeline monitoring crews. The study was now in effect being funded by Alyeska Pipeline Service Company itself, the oil company consortium that is building the eight-hundred-mile Pipeline

from Prudhoe Bay on the North Slope to the tank farm on Dayville Flats.

George and Al finished the day's collecting in the flats and headed over to check on the number of salmon started on their way upstream. It was only the second day they had been running. Upon reaching the mudflat access road, now under construction as a land route to the Terminal site, the two men watched a project engineer hesitate a moment by his pickup and then stride up to them.

"I took two pictures, George, just to show you that clay we hit down there, why there was no way to keep those culverts in, it would just have buckled in the middle, so I was thinking of you all along, yessir, and took these photos to show you what it was like." George, a country boy from Kentucky who kept his mild manner and easy ways; George is a good listener, and heard the engineer out. They walked together to the metal culvert that allowed the stream to pass beneath the new road, and surveyed the stagnant pool on the upstream side. The eighteen-inch culvert was placed about two-and-a-half feet above the water level, forcing the freshwater to back up and drop all the vital nutrients it carried for the tidewater flats and the clams below. It was no longer a stream; it couldn't reach the sea.

It was George's responsibility to oversee the Terminal operations for the Marine Fisheries Service, so he patiently explained to the project engineer that "one thousand pink and chum salmon spawned in this stream in 1971, three years back. The blueprints and specs call for a four-foot culvert, Roger, and this one's only eighteen inches. . . . And all of those salmon are probably going to have difficulty coming up a barely trickling stream to jump three feet in the air and shoot through a twenty-two-foot galvanized pipe into the squalid pond on the other side. You've got to do something fast, Roger, none of the salmon will make it. They're running hard now."

Roger suggested that they could fill in the stream and try diking both sides to encourage the flow. At the moment, they were out of four-foot culverts. "Maybe build a concrete sluice for the stream," Roger continued slowly, as all three men watched six or seven raw-

meat-pink arcs of light splash in the faint waters on the downstream side of the road. "Hell, I don't know anything about fish, but we'll try to do something in the next day or two. But we got to get in another hundred feet of fill and grade it by tomorrow morning to stay on schedule, that's all I know."

Chilkoot Charlie's bar in Fairbanks was a lively open door on the carnival all-night summer madness in Alaska. Fire fighters spun yarns in one corner; river rats planned epic two-month trips down the fiercest whitewater in North America, the Alsek River through the St. Elias Mountains to the southeast; Pipeliners jawboned full of spit, lacking polish. The Pipeline was the drawing card now, after all. Money, helicopters, aggressive hookers, gambling on the sly, artful con men, enormous machinery devouring the land, and deep drafts of the silent wildness: Down at Tommies, buying your way into the union isn't too bad, I hear, maybe five hundred. . . . But union C cards are good enough to get on now, dude, you best get your tail in gear. . . . Local Hire don't mean shit, really. . . . Keep your eyes on those pipe welders, the 798ers from Tulsa? Man, they're a mean crowd, goddamn red-necks, just as soon fight as piss. . . .

A short, wiry young man in blue jeans and a ragged denim jacket, cheeks bearing the scars of what looked like smallpox, wiped off his three-day growth with a crumpled red bandanna as he walked by once again. Third time now. A massive bearded man in embroidered overalls, with one silver earring, roared a wrath of obscenities to no one special at peak volume, something about what the son of some mongrel he knew could do with various carefully specified parts of his anatomy.

Flash, tussle, beer surging like a tidal bore across the table, chairs in splinters on the floor. "What the fuck are you doing with my wallet, goddamn it! You stupid ass! . . ." Warren, who had been quietly sipping nearby, kept smashing the wiry blemished dude into a stocky spruce post. The timber shuddered each time; the figure wrapped in denim said nothing. No one paid much attention. Khumpp, khhoaap! the pickpocket's chest expired with each blow in a resounding chant. Finally, a couple of clean-cut drugstore cowboys wrestled raving Warren away, still screaming at the pickpocket now gasping facedown on the table, soaked in sweat and Olympia beer. The band had begun another electric blues number; everyone kept on drinking and randomly giving Rebel yells. A barmaid tipped the table over to drain the beer, and set it up for the people still there, once the bouncer had unloaded the troublemaker from the tabletop.

Warren started to relax to his usual laid-back self as a couple of his evening's drinking buddies got him outside into First Avenue's northern air. They all walked to the parking lot on the opposite side of the sludgy Chena River, and sat on the grass with brown-bagged wine and animated conversation. Travelers talk long and well, as all of their stories are fresh and need fit only their own design. A bald man with sunglasses — even at two A.M. the sun was bright — and a German shepherd slowly walked by and carefully assessed the collective, but they'd already heard about the "narc" who frequented the river area and checked for drugs. Word travels fast when everyone lies in wait.

The conversation shifted to all the usual subjects, away from the fight and the narcs. Someone mentioned that he'd heard that twenty-three workers were currently on strike at Happy Valley camp up on the North Slope, north of the Brooks Range, and north of about everything else. The strike concerned food, sure, that made sense. Only they were striking because the menu was too boring there, they wanted variety: too much steak, five meals a week, someone said, five! The walkout's consequence was more hamburger at "Giggly Gulch."

Warren and the boys walked through the municipal parking lot past homemade rigs and license plates exploring every variation on the theme, most of which had recently navigated the muddy or dusty or bone-jarring Alaska Highway, depending on whom one talked to. There wasn't much else to do beyond move on to another bar, so a couple of suggestions were

Anchorage

Job call at Laborers Union

Family from North Carolina

thrown out. Let's see, there's the Savoy, if we want a little serious Native night life, and maybe death, hey that place is pretty heavy! . . . You hear about that dude the other night who got knifed in there for grabbing that Indian girl's ass? Right in the belly, no preambles or arguments or nothing, just zambo . . . the woman's friend was really totaled; somebody said he just came in from Fort Yukon to try and take her back to the village, I dunno, that's what I heard. Where the hell *is* Fort Yukon? . . . Or we could sashay on down to Tommy's Elbow Room and find out who crashed on the landing strip yesterday; that's where all the giant Herc pilots hang out — naw, the pilots aren't so big, but the planes are something else! Those guys fly incredible quantities of supplies and stuff up to the camps north of the Yukon every day in unbelievable weather, fog and hellacious big mountains with snow on them and all kinds of shit. . . . So the day after a crash, the place'll be hopping. . . .

While Valdez is just beginning to learn all over again in its dazzling fjord and ingenuous trailer park streets, Fairbanks has laid a boom's tracks and squandered its wealth before. Like any free port linking a bountiful land and trade routes to the outside, Fairbanks was at once the location of the intense activity of the working, and the penetrating restlessness of those who lie in wait. In coldest Fairbanks, the winter is hard and wears people thin. They become either very good — or very poor — at waiting.

Finally, after a look in the Savoy on Second Avenue, the crew moved on to the Chena Bar, down in the same block. The Chena is the major Native bar in town, bare cinder block, a prominent neon sign and swooping arrow that hasn't worked in years, and the grossly faded "Wanted Native Band" sign that has hung in the window unaltered beyond anyone's remembrance. An all-Native band was playing loud, spacy rock music as they went in, a drifting-snow sound that soared on and on in a lazy yet vaguely transcendental way. They were from Kotzebue, out on the Bering Sea coast, one woman at the bar thought, her friend said Barrow; no one was sure. The cavern-dark dance floor was crowded with enthusiastic young Eskimos and Indians, and a

score of ebullient army recruits on leave who somehow escaped the tranquil offerings of the log cabin USO club up on First Avenue. A Canadian Eskimo from Inuvik, on the McKenzie River, threw out theories about Greenlander sculpture, Danish colonialism there, and a Swedish organist who set the J. R. R. Tolkien trilogy to mad flights of music. Drifting thick smoke, constant clashes, raw and unrefined energy, the place was an Alaskan version of a hard core Harlem jazz bar in the fifties.

A very short and compact Eskimo woman — "it's better to be stocky like that in the cold, plenty of insulation" — fell off the stool next to Warren and lay on the filthy floor without moving. Warren laughed knowingly, and said he understood how she felt. A barmaid and then a customer tripped over her before another Native woman came over, admonished her soundly, and picked her up clumsily, though lovingly. Her glazed expression never changed throughout. People in the Chena were generally amiable drunks. The Eskimo and Indian personalities were gentle and centered enough so that when the desired state of total inebriation arrived, a casual, timid withdrawal occurred, not the blind bitterness of new arrivals from the South and West, the ones who left everything behind.

Warren, a carpenter, began to talk of his stay in Alaska so far. A friend had decided to leave San Francisco in the late winter "to make the big money, so I said I'm going too, and that was it. I'm a union member, but for the last two years, I've just been scabbing out, just trying to stay alive. There are literally thousands of carpenters in 'Frisco, and basically no work at all.

"It took us like fourteen days to get up here. We've had it pretty tough. We're traveling on a slim financial budget. We have a '53 Chevy eighteen-foot flatbed truck, and it's, like, maintenance hassles; every day at least two hours keeping it in running condition. And the Alaska Highway has been pretty tough on us. We went through two generators, and it was forty bucks for a twenty-dollar generator. Neither of us are mechanics, but you learn things pretty fast when your truck is broke down forty miles from the nearest town and it's twenty below zero out in a snowstorm. We don't have a

heater in the truck either. So when we were traveling along at forty to fifty miles an hour and it might be twenty below zero out, the wind chill was like eighty below zero inside the truck. So, like, we were in sleeping bags while we were driving."

Warren had another Coke on the rocks, a vegetarian who never drank liquor, he awkwardly explained. His unruly cocoa-colored hair and darker beard obscured the lines of his face, and most of the expression they might contain. The facial muscles still visible were all concisely drawn taut, each one separately arranged in a formal pose, like a plaster of paris death mask.

"We had to travel at night and sleep during the day because we had a bad battery, and the truck could never start in the morning. That became a bit of a hassle because gas stations are sometimes a hundred miles apart and it's almost impossible to catch them open at night. . . . We slept at night in a camper that we built onto the back of the truck, three feet wide, six feet tall, and ten foot long, with a wood-burning stove in the back, and we carried oak firewood to keep warm. Nothing but drifting snow everywhere. The stove saved my feet one night. . . ." The band began another set suddenly, with a high whining guitar solo that burst into a driving rhythm when the drummer and bassist joined in. A short, crewcut Native wearing glasses collided with the white barmaid; bottled beer smashed on the floor and ran down his dark blue nylon windbreaker, across its "Arctic Village, Alaska" white block lettering.

"We had just crossed a bridge and gone up an icy hill," Warren suddenly injected, "and we broke down at the top of the hill, on a curve, and in the few minutes it took to get the truck pushed to a safe spot, I completely lost feeling in both my feet from the extreme cold and wind. We got a fire going as fast as we could . . . and our gas mileage was down to five miles a gallon on that road, and to make it worse, the gas went up in price. We paid as much as ninety-eight cents a gallon. We had no idea it would cost that much, and left 'Frisco with about three hundred and fifty dollars apiece, figuring that was plenty. Between us we've got about six and a half bucks now. After our second day on the Alcan at 'Mile Post 500' we figured out that we didn't think we were going to make it, with our lousy gas mileage, so we absolutely couldn't spend money on anything but gasoline and oil. But once you get about six hundred miles down the road, everyone realizes that they're all headed to Alaska, and they're all dependent on each other . . ."

The one thing that concerned them most was the two thousand dollars' worth of carpenter's tools in the truck, "so there was no way we were going to abandon it. We would sooner freeze to death and die in it. It's pretty weird. It looks like a real wreck, but to us right now, it's life." In the smoky, ruckus room Warren's dense, dark face absorbed light without reflecting it, as if still in a state of extreme retraction from the searing cold.

"We got some amazing looks coming up here when we were on the Alcan, like dust bowl Okies headed to California in the Depression. People would look at us, about break their necks trying to turn around to see who in the hell was getting out of that wreck. People would be hitchhiking, it might be twenty-below out, nothing but frozen whiteness everywhere, they'd look at us coming down the road and just put their thumb away. This one guy we helped had run out of gas, so we backed down the road to his truck and got out. They were just looking at us and you could feel that they were just weirded out. You knew they must have been thinking Charles Manson, and the whole bit; you know, California plates, two bearded burnouts climbing out of this thing that looks like a truck. They were really scared, and were picturing the headlines in tomorrow's papers. Granny was shaking and the little girls were sort of cringing by the side of their truck. The guy tried to give Jim a ten dollar bill for three dollars' worth of gas, but we just said we hope someone does the same for us if we are stuck. That really shook him up because he knew he would never stop for us. . . ."

One of the people at the table had just come off the Line, up north of Fairbanks at Livengood camp, and got up to indulge in a game of rowdy pool. He wandered over to the ragged felt table, grabbed a cue that was missing the leather tip, then sauntered back to consult with the others. "Hey, listen! I'll get this round for yah all, how's that. . . . And, say, will you jist watch my coat, will yah? Got mah paychecks and fifteen hundred

in cash in that there coat pocket, so jist watch mah coat. . . .'' He went back to the pool area, muttering something about earning "fourteen thousand dollars clear'' — after taxes — for a ten-week stint in Livengood, "driving pipe trucks on the Kamikaze Trail.''

Warren was still in town though, waiting. He came up in early May in the first few weeks after work on the Pipeline had actually begun, "after all the delays and court battles and whatever the hell else held them up.'' Like a lot of people in town, he'd heard of the amazing wages from his sister-in-law's ex-boyfriend's barber, and hoped something would break. The Carpenters Union was filled with aspirants; they'd already sold the hydraulic jack and spare tires on the truck, waiting. For now, they stayed in the campground down by the Chena River bridge, the huge Hercs roaring overhead all through the sunlit non-night from the airport close by, headed for the stillness, the sterility of the Slope.

The Fairbanks Rescue Mission became home for a while when funds ran out completely and it was still below zero at night. Free meals were available if one suffered through the service from seven until eight-thirty every evening, rewarded by a plate of "some kind of pretty weird looking stew, real strong smell, maybe caribou meat or something, and big chunks of boiled cabbage and radishes.'' They'd taken a shower there the first night to save the dollar charge at the YMCA. The shower was both a urinal and a brewery. There was always a crowd of local Native winos there, passing a bottle around in the only spot in the mission safe from the omniscient maternal eye of the ageless matron who hammered away on the piano and was thoroughly in charge of the singing at the services.

One Eskimo in particular always camped out in the bathroom, constantly mumbling to himself. He approached each entrant and shook his hand and told him his name about six different times, each time with slight variation. The complete iconography of some uncertain faith hung heavily from his neck and belt; a well-abused Gideon's Bible he kissed ceremoniously was constant companion and surrogate lover. During the services, he would vigorously lead the hymns before returning to the bathroom. Another of the seventy or so men who attended most services would generally be gagging and blowing lunch in the back, where those who sought to sleep through the sermons usually congregated. An Aleut from Unalaska, out in the Aleutian Islands, had secured permanent status in the mission by contributing help in the kitchen; during each service he sat and mumbled aloud, "Who the hell is this Jesus? Where *is* that fucker?'' before returning to the dishes. It was his daily role, almost a directed response to the administered sacraments. Each day another group of indigent Pipeline hopefuls would swell the mission's ranks, and trade off the few available roles of drunk, mumbler, and pious stoic with the corps of entrenched mission regulars.

The band's foreign mood, a dimensionless blizzard of sound, suddenly ceased in mid-song. They quickly packed their instruments and were instantly led from the stage and out the front door by two Alaska State Troopers in fur hats. No explanations; no one knew why; no questions remained after about four or five minutes of initial interest. But there was always plenty of beer, at a buck and a half a bottle.

"So the hiring hall is a good place to pick up women, if not jobs. Had pretty good luck there; the ladies are all just desperate and looking for work and a place to stay, and pretty feisty women, a lot of fun. But six-fifty isn't going to last long," Bill continued, "so I'm going to sell some of my blood tomorrow. That's really why no beer tonight, though I am a vegetarian. I got the rarest blood in the world, AB negative or positive, I'm not sure which, but only Indians have it usually. I figure I can off a pint or two for some good bread, until the Pipe job comes through. This is the chance of a lifetime for me to make it, the only thing left . . ."

Valdez camp

Where the
Mountains Break the Back of the Sea

Valdez is a bit startling at first. So splendid a fairytale cove would warrant National Park status anywhere but Alaska. But most of the time its residents must rely on faith and memory of the way it was before those clouds moved in, for they see only the braided threads of streams cast down into the sea from the low hemlines of rainclouds. The fjords certainly excited the Aleut and Tlingit traders who passed through, and in 1790 charmed Salvador Fidalgo into bestowing the name of his superior back in Spain, Antonio Valdez, minister of marine, onto the bay.

Valdez is a bit startling, always. Can this really be the fabled town of gold rush sagas, tales of mushing north on the Richardson Trail to the mineral-rich Interior? There is no grass in Valdez, virtually anywhere. The old fishing village of the same name was completely destroyed by the Good Friday earthquake of 1964. The relocated, rebuilt town consists of one enormous gravel pad strewn with rows of prefab units, separated by streets identifiable only by the patterned absence of trailers. It looks as if the traveling circus has at last arrived for the late summer county fair, and its city of carnival delights and accompanying sadness has sprung up in the vacant fairground overnight. No one knows how long it will stay.

The rain never even tries to leave. And there is some madness at work, round the clock at that, fashioning a few simple peaks and the bays they've captured from the sea into a shining metallic Terminal on the ocean's edge. On bedrock shelves and steel pilings, a radiant city of oil tanks and valves carefully gauged, and computers, and again, another set of oil fields encased in steel plate, great swaths of iron already tinted rust by the sea salt air. And supertanker berths, spots to sleep and recover from the long, stormy voyage north, places to gorge themselves on the always flowing oil.

There is an intense history of voyaging north along the Inland Passage, hiding behind the granite and spruce islands from the scuttling commotion of the Gulf of Alaska's storms, thrown against humble Tlingit Indian war canoes and fragile Spanish, Russian and American colonial dreams of conquest and discovery. The Japanese current sweeps up the Aleutian Islands from distant Asia, its wild warmth both assaulting and simmering the thin coastal strip between arrogant mountains and the sea. Tufted puffins, lava-black sea birds with tropical orange beaks, fly in the current's winds like box kites from China; whale and sea lion swim below. This is the route the supertankers will take too, when they leave Valdez laden with Alaskan crude and fly south with the puffins; or sail west to Japan, where the current and pipe both began.

Port Valdez — deepest waters in a blue so dark it grades into black, rimmed by stark raving mad mountains — is a vivid remembrance of how the world once was, still wet from birth. On a rainy afternoon, Valdez becomes gray. The generators across the bay at the Terminal hum and the lights glow, and the port becomes another Halifax, one more Edinburgh.

The impressive town-sized Anderson Glacier descends directly toward the Perkins family's two-room cabin from the west. There's no danger, though, because the azure ice field is a few miles away, across a moat of deepest Port Valdez waters. It's the centerpiece of their tiny homestead, visible from one of their few small windows — glass is a luxury in cabins, and comes later on when there's a little more money and time available. George Perkins is an avid mountaineer and, with his wife Joan and their two young girls, Amy and Eileen, spends weekends away from the mudflat *Macoma inconspicua* clams, climbing the ripsaw peaks that encircle Port Valdez.

George — tall, lanky, slow-talking, dressed in wool shirts or salt-and-pepper wool jacket — had located his homesite about five years earlier, while cross-country skiing one winter afternoon to escape the confines of life teaching natural science at Valdez High School. It was snowing heavily, the huge, fluffy wind-driven flakes characteristic of humid areas and temperatures not far below freezing. George ducked down over a knoll into a tiny cove that faced west to the open seas and was completely free of the blasts coming off Valdez Glacier and Thompson Pass to the east. After a few hours there, he decided that would be the spot, if ever he were to build a home.

Brunet, enthusiastic Joan Perkins was a bilingual tour guide for the hotels in Mount McKinley National Park and took to spending time with George, then a resident park ranger. After a later stint together in Glacier Bay National Monument, near Juneau in "Southeast" Alaska, Joan joined George permanently in his one-room cabin on the special spot pointed out in storm, years before. Now, George is doing whatever odd jobs come his way, in spite of his graduate training in physics. A few years back, he taught full-time in Valdez, then only part-time, before having a brabble with the new principal over a variety of differences. He decided against teaching the next year and became the school's janitor; worked as a technical assistant on an oceanographic study of the local ecosystem for the University of Alaska; joined the weather service as an observer, a classic Alaskan Bush job with fair pay and light responsibilities; and then went with Marine Fisheries to do fieldwork on the "tiny thumbnail-sized clams." George always unconsciously measured off their actual dimensions when discussing the clams, by holding up his left thumb, so that it isolated the oval right thumbnail, usually dark with outboard oil or grime. It's tough to stay scrubbed clean in a cabin without running water, plumbing, or stove, and hardly matters anyhow.

Joan was working on the aluminum camping pot that had suffered injury in the previous night's tuna, noodle and cheese stew. The girls had been dressed in their long underwear, dresses, rain gear and life jackets for the twenty-minute open boat ride into town.

George fiddled with a new mantle for the Coleman lantern but lit the kerosene Aladdin lamp instead, to illuminate a seminal report on Alaskan historical geology written in the 1930's by Alfred Hulse Brooks, the pioneer scientist and author. The running monologue by Joan continued on "Education 693," a sixteen-hour mini-course on "Oil in Alaska" offered as a teacher education class at Southeastern Senior College in the fall of 1973, the previous year. She was well known around town as a resident firebrand capable of impassioned, impromptu speeches on a variety of subjects from education to citizens' rights, but environmental topics were her forte. Local officials were amused or enchanted to see an attractive, freckled woman of about thirty years rise at public meetings, until they were under eloquent, unswerving fire. "So the course in Juneau . . . only three texts — two published by the American Petroleum Institute, the third by the American Association of Oil-well Drilling Contractors, whoever they are — twelve speakers, all but one employed by oil or related industries . . . imagine! That was the course, no comment from any other parties who might have another view, and that's not . . ." Joan trailed off and studied several jars of new specimens of plants and sea life they'd recently collected. The cabin was stuffed with natural sciences books and handsome rocks from all over the bay.

Everyone got a little wet on the way into town. The surf was high and the twenty-foot boat took twice the usual time, slapping slate waves and casting fine salt sea spray, amid the outrageous white flashes of glaciers hidden high in the flow of a storm front.

Joe was driving a D-9 cat, clearing a dense cottonwood forest. The D-9 is the largest bulldozer made. An entire herd was employed in Valdez to transform the gravel bar forest and graywacke stone shores into shapes and sizes appropriate for the oversized building block pieces of the Terminal. Joe would rather operate the front-end loader placing culverts in ditches, but the Operators Union steward had told him to keep his mouth shut and stick with the D-9 for another couple days. The loader operator did very little; there was very little to do. "Hey!" was the regular call from friends, "we've got a Pipeline to build!" And the usual response, "What Pipeline?" Whenever the boss was around in the characteristic Alyeska canary-yellow pickup, the loader seemed raring to go, black exhaust smoke unsuppressed by the continuous drizzle. As he pulled away, the operator would again watch for ducks.

There are plenty of birds in Valdez, all through the bountiful mudflats, marshes, forests. There are plenty of black bear and all sorts of other critters, too. So every so often, the operator would look up from his slumbers awaiting another culvert or Alyeska timekeeper, spot some ducks, and reach into the pickup for his twelve-gauge shotgun and blast away twice into the sky, walk over and throw the unlucky ducks into the truck and return to his dreams, never saying a word.

Joe really wanted the job. He'd left his wife and kids behind in their new trailer in Iowa City to try to get on the Pipeline. All day long, he would sit on the cat and muse about his firstborn's first days in second grade, though apparently she didn't hate it as much now as initially, according to his wife's letters. But he wondered what Dorie had meant when she said that he shouldn't make a special effort to come home on his next R and R. Everyone in camp had a story or two of men who sent big checks home every week or two, and then arrived there to find that their wives had simply moved out of the house, with no forwarding address.

Joe had loads of second thoughts about traveling north to Alaska. At lunch, it was a regular topic. "The whole damned show here isn't what it was cracked up to be . . . all that hype from Alyeska, glossy brochures about the great project, *Alaska, the last frontier, represents a new challenge to the pioneering instinct in the American people,* yeah, that was it, and other bullshit." Another cat operator agreed with Joe; most of them did.

"All those pretty pictures and I ain't seen a mountain here in two weeks. Big talk — *The $6.4 billion trans*

Alaska pipeline is the largest privately financed project in the history of the world . . . and also one of the most challenging construction efforts in history. No women, nothing but rain and rot. Only the money, no other reason to be here . . ."

Joe adjusted the earphones worn under his hard hat to ward off the noise, another OSHA requirement for the worker's safety. He fooled with the stereo tape deck that the earphones were furtively plugged into, pulled out the Waylon Jennings tape and replaced it with one by Tanya Tucker, crooning about that tall, lean man who turned her mama on.

The enormous bulldozer chopped into the grove of cottonwood again, steel burnished by many thousand strokes ripping the bark and fiber of shade trees. Permanent townhouses for Alyeska and subcontractor management were planned to go up due west of town and not far from George Perkins's cabin. The entire area was clear cut; it looked like the seven o'clock news of the latest jungle fighting in the Central Highlands of Vietnam.

Joe's experience bore out the other operator's complaint. It wasn't like it was billed. There had been a mandatory orientation session run by Alyeska in Fairbanks and Anchorage, a full day of classes for all Pipeline workers on Project History, Safety, Environ-

ment, Human Relations, and the Camps, one day required by the Project Agreement to acquaint workers with the unique ecological and historical situation in Alaska. The project had been controversial from the beginning, because some environmentalists are not too open-minded, and some Natives are worried, too, he had been told by a blond Alyeskan named Pat. But it had resulted in a stronger, better pipeline, she felt, as a result of those questions that kept the project from starting for a good five years, tied up in federal courts by the Sierra Club. Orientation was exactly like the army, rows of forms and people and rules. There had been a lot of talk about permafrost, a mixture of rock, gravel, silt and ice that remains at temperatures below thirty-two degrees F. They had told him to be real careful about all the environmental regulations and inspectors, and to just grin and bear it, but it was just tearing down a forest as usual, get it out of there. Knock down another soft cottonwood, chain drag it to the pile, sheaths of spongy bark stripped off, a molting forest so prefab houses could grow. No, not grow, nothing grows from the soil these days; they just bring in the ready-made parts and bolt them all together. Joe unplugged the earphones and got on the bus heading back to camp for dinner, his twelve hours' worth over.

The temporary work camp was erected in a canyon just north and east of town, a few miles below the terminus of the Valdez Glacier. This was a bit of a joke around town, because any fool knew that in winter the area out around the ramshackle, tar papered airport was the windiest place this side of Patagonia. Yet it was a spot blessed with its share of the meager local lore. In Alaska, there's usually not enough history to go around. Somehow the architects of the project had an uncanny comprehension of the past and laid their plans with a general storekeeper's sense of local history.

The camp had been erected by barging prefab trailer units constructed in Seattle up to Valdez and hauling the rest of the equipment hundreds of miles from Anchor-

age over slick mountain roads. About twelve hundred men and a handful of women crammed into row after row of connected units, two to a room, the same colors repeated ad nauseam. Pickups and cars of every shape were parked outside in the gravel and mud, while the workers tried to wash off the day's trials with hot water inside. The rain was everywhere. No gear made, not even the favored Helly Hanson Norwegian sea parkas, could fend it off all day. No matter what the weather, everyone had to pretend to work to keep their boss, and his boss, and the timekeepers, and the timekeepers who watched the timekeepers, out of trouble with whoever was at the top. The rooms draped themselves in humid sweat as all the gear was hung up to dry, the stench

carefully circulated around the camp by the ventilation system. Foot powder, constant coughs, deep colds and flannel mouth were the symptoms of what was known as "Val-disease," and no one was exempt from it. An entire tin and fiberboard company town thrown up for the workers, like around the steel mills in Birmingham in Walker Evans's photographs from the thirties.

A couple of the boys new to the camp wandered out late on a summer night to explore. It was the first glacier they'd seen, as ice fields are fairly scarce around L.A., and a couple of six packs had convinced them of the necessity of visiting it firsthand. Even at one A.M. it was light enough to drive past the city campground in a Fluor crewcab and set out on uncertain feet for the glowing ice. The approach was blocked by a sizable iceberg-filled lake dammed behind the terminal moraine, so the pair stripped and desperately swam the outlet stream roaring through a single breech over polished ice. After crossing another icy strait, moving barefoot on a pebbly ice island, they realized it would take four more exhaustingly cold crossings just to reach the main ice-floe. Two startled, staggering wide-eyed infants raged across the swift current that sought to take them in its sway, and crawled ashore unable to walk on blued, exploded feet. They uncontrollably bellowed more air for insatiable lungs.

The routine of life was simple. Work "seven-twelves," or a week straight of twelve-hour days, then back to the luxury of a shower and meal before beginning the normal night of some combination of pool, movies, letter writing, jawboning, and hustling.

The Club Valdez, the Glacier Bar, the Pipeliner — all the bars in town were packed on the Fourth of July. Somebody had arranged to shoot off fireworks over Port Valdez, and the whole town was lining the small boat-harbor in various states of inebriation and opiated disarray, blasting music and spitting gravel on all the other new campers and Blazers and pickups as they sped off elsewhere. Hank was moving slowly to another booth to avoid the partying in his last one, to finish his second steak. It was his standard policy to order three steaks every Wednesday and Saturday, one rare, one medium, and one well-done. Figured that was the only way to get one just right, and ritually threw out the other two, each time. But tonight was one of those gray times when a man just sits and keeps stuffing himself, drinking coffee, forgetting, marinating in caffeine.

Hank, a loner, wandered over to the Glacier Bar and watched the dance of holiday there. A special Fourth of July band was rocking the house, despite its modest appearance: two guitarists and a tape recorder. One musician simply sat on the windowsill and offered a bass rhythm, while the lead guitarist fiddled with the tapes to get a suitable snare-drum beat to embellish with his predictable, mechanized melodies. Everyone was too drunk to chaff at the only live music in town; it was too loud to hear it clearly anyway.

Another round of firecrackers went off under one of the tables, knocking over several patrons in Olympia Beer golf hats made of plastic beer labels stitched together with heavy red yarn. They collided with a crew of grizzly codgers still sporting their Fluor hard hats after hours, and the potential flare-up faded into a mock gladiator duel between the two biggest men, one swinging his tar-stained denim jacket like a fighter's fishnet, to trip the other. Restraint; it had to be there. The specter of violent total ruin from all those haggard men hung ever in the air, and scared even the hungriest among them. "Ahh, the round's on me, what the hell, got a fat wad today, you know, like aww always say, sometimes aww've got some money and then, well, aww take care of mah friends. Yeah, we look after each other, right?"

There was some hard-hatted determination toward a local lady, already married off but not ineligible for less long-term obligations. One of the stalwarts at the bar winked to Hank, adding that "this here Pipeline has made the place a lady's choice town, and been somewhat hard on the Valdez High girls, but all things considered, the women in town, they've been pretty good sports about it so far . . ."

Trailer park in Anchorage

Mail call

A camp secretary

Hank went back to the gold carpeted trailer in camp that he called home, amidst miles of aisles of carpet in gold, and sat sadly immersed in a Kris Kristofferson song about a woman named Bobby McGee who'd slipped away. During the seven-month wait in Anchorage while trying to get on the Line, he had written a note on shirt cardboard and taped it on his black '56 Ford Fairlane: *Looking for Female — To have a baby: We will live together for the time necessary to produce a child. I also plan to get in the Union, the proceeds to help support the little bastard — let's share a wounderful year together — I enjoy motorcycles, racing cars movies, bowling, picnics, etc. If serious call . . .* The number had been scratched out, and replaced with, *Ask for Hank, leave phone no. PS I have a couch and refrigerator and a queen bed for a start.* It hadn't worked.

Over at the Terminal site, heroic things were going on. A permanent camp for 2800 workers was partially constructed from more prefab units placed in fifteen parallel lines on the steep slope. Enormous white structures, situated as a rocky redoubt above the gray bay, they gave the site the look of a penal colony, a stuccoed-white forced-labor camp on a distant isle, exiled from memory. One island in an archipelago of several dozen bright white camps stretching north through the tundra and taiga to Prudhoe Bay, homes for expatriots from myriad pasts, mirrored in eyes of glass.

Thousands of men worked two shifts around the clock, traveling back and forth on the Kathelynn, a ferry brought up from Seattle until the access road was completed. Then buses took over, hauling the help to the site, to a barbed-wire gate where each man had to present his ID and "brass in" — pick up his numbered brass tag — with the timekeepers. The buses reloaded on the inside and drove the men up a steep grade to the actual tank farm site, where men served their time on bedrock terraces sculpted from a mountain that had become a terraced rice paddy hill in the tropics, planted with coffers of steel in beds of concrete.

They blasted out platforms for the eighteen storage tanks, three ballast water treatment tanks for the supertankers, a 37.5 megawatt power plant, fifty-six buildings, and miles of interconnected oil, water and utility pipes leading to one floating and three fixed berths for the over 165,000 deadweight ton tankers. The 1000-acre Terminal site is the largest camp on the Pipeline, employing up to 4000 workers to move and rearrange 13 million cubic yards of rock. The Terminal will cost $1 billion, and will expend roughly 10.5 million man-hours of labor.

The 510,000-barrel welded-steel tanks, eighteen now and thirty-two eventually, each 250 feet in diameter, rest on reinforced concrete set onto bedrock to resist earthquakes like the 8.6 Richter scale quake in '64 that had its epicenter near Valdez and leveled the town. It would cost $3 million to remove the thirty feet of snow of the winter coming up, in order to keep work on schedule. Three 430,000-barrel ballast treatment tanks will rise 62 feet. A 300-foot smokestack was barged to Valdez in two pieces and erected by a crane capable of lifting its 420-ton mass. Each fixed berth for the tankers will cost about $45 million and is anchored in 100-foot-deep bedrock; a fourth berth measuring 387 by 96 feet will float in the 160-foot-deep water after being shipped from Japan by barges, which will be sunk in order to launch it.

There have been relatively few things built of steel in Alaska, for its suggestion of immutability and stability somehow rings false in a land beset by magic, where men are visitors with visas that need constant renewal by faith and perseverance. Steel has come from somewhere else, and if it lasts, the planks and Ashley stoves will go. But the water brings rust, and the earth moves dramatically whenever it pleases, so we shall see.

47

He couldn't have seen anything out the tiny window, not a thing. It was too fogged by the condensation from within, and the full-blown wetness brought across the swelling sea right outside. But George was a lost voyager in that single pane of glass as if in quest of a vision; it was only the smell of burned salmon that reminded him that he hadn't stirred enough.

The Perkinses were preparing a large salmon that friend Randy had caught in the clear bay a few hours earlier. Conversation was strained because of the melancholy dampness that filled the log room, and due to the roar of the two Optimus backpacking stoves struggling to boil potatoes and sauté fish. Joan was telling a favorite story about their effort to obtain a lease on their land. Five years earlier the city of Valdez had sent someone out to assess the plot and cabin. Joan figured it would only be one more year before the town broke even on the place through taxes, as the assessor had to hire a boat to get out there and back and computed a very low value. But adjacent waterfront land had recently sold for $1500 an acre, and no former values were stable. It was a gnawing burden to keep up on developments; each day offered novelty.

George had been in to the high school not long before to give a talk on the oceanographic research done in Port Valdez beginning in May 1971. He told Randy of his illustrated and involved lecture while mixing powdered milk in a large glass jar. The first question asked after the lecture, one posed by the son of a contractor in town, was "How much do you make as a biologist?" He laughed as best he could, and shook the jar vigorously, turning powder into foam.

George Perkins had climbed onto the Valdez Glacier himself, and returned with an odd assortment of debris: parched shoe soles, broken barrel staves, a collapsible top hat still intact. Valdez was a major port city for seekers rushing north to the Fairbanks goldfields just after the turn of the century, and the route over the three icefalls on the glacier took quite a toll of men, material, and lust. Hazards — chasms, avalanches, sheer-rock faces — guarded all the entrances to the wealth of the Interior. Another route was pushed up Keystone Canyon, a miraculous cleft in the urn of mountains surrounding the harbor. The original plans had called for the Pipeline's passage through this dark, wet secret of a gorge, but the pressures brought to bear by the state monitors due to its scenic splendor had forced Alyeska to reroute the pipe out of sight.

In another year, 1907, a fight over the use of the canyon had erupted into gunfire. Two rival railroad companies sponsored by Eastern money had been vying for first passage through the gorge, considered the key to the Interior. Their track and survey crews had gotten into a fight that ended in one death; a major trial called attention to the situation, and led to the abandonment of the route by both companies. The Copper River and Northwestern Railroad went north to the McCarthy copper fields from the fledgling port of Katalla, and then from Cordova when the artificial breakwater of the first port failed to resist the fury of the sea.

Valdez is an outpost town on the frontier, with all that that means — all of the blatant greed of regular folk with the strong, slender fingers of pickpockets and concert pianists, doing numbers with a hard lead pencil; adjusting a hat against the wind. The myriad young men, the women, with roving ambition fleeing from a past still in pursuit, or buoyed by gigantic ideas. All the women with nowhere else to go; the sons on inheritance. The pool halls full of artful stories of one's past arrayed around an avoidance of one's future.

History can be the cruelest of kings; it both guides and deceives. History as fresh as it is in Alaska is still oral and fabled, not yet the dogma of accurate historical accounts, so everyone is entitled to his personal interpretation based on the individual's distance from the events and the persons involved in them. There is a beauty to this egalitarian, socialized history free of experts and elites, in which everyone participates, but it is marred by the concomitant tragedy of mythologizing. Events too fresh lack in perspective. They are not yet tied to the consequences they bring to bear on their perpetrators; there are causes without effects. Alaska has seen only three or four generations play out their time on her land, and they have done so with but few neighbors, so the parables and lessons are scarce. Space is lord in Alaska, room to move around in without judgment from

Casualty at Valdez

another. Judgments are suspended or forgotten in such a land, where all live as innocents again, with no constraints on the forms their lives may take. But once the pioneers encounter each other more and more as growth diminishes the frontier, some change in perspective occurs, the sense of aloneness has to give way to a collective view of the whole system.

George and Joan sat out on the gravel beach in front of the cabin watching the Anderson Glacier move in and out of the mists across the way. The Perkinses are astute naturalists carefully studying the world they live in, collecting samples of unknown flora and fauna on weekend trips into the surrounding peaks, and lining the shelves of the cabin with these questions. The idea of plant succession and recolonization was of particular interest, because they had spent much time in Glacier Bay, site of some of the most important work in that field. As the glaciers rapidly retreated they left behind gravel deposits suddenly open to competition among various species to fill the ecological niche. Mosses, perennial herbs and willow formed the pioneer community that arrived first to colonize an area recently vacated by ice; Joan joked about their being the driven innovators, the ones that loved any new scene, the foot-loose adventurers, people who want to scrawl their names in setting concrete. Willow and alder thickets occupied areas adjacent to the pioneer plant communities and followed them as a second wave; they became the slightly more hesitant and cautious group that needed to get their roots in and make a fairly solid commitment, "kind of middle class, you might say, reliable, the hard workers." The conifer forests of hemlock and Sitka spruce comprised the third stage of colonization and eventually outcompeted the other two communities if they could get a foothold in an area. Sometimes the alders and willows were too well entrenched, and "the conifers were just a little too late to get in on the action, never quite got started up toward the retreating glaciers, but stayed near the shores of the bays and the ocean." They wondered if the accumulation of all those near-misses ever got to them, one more misty opportunity that never came to be. In a way it was sad to think about whole species that one could tell would never make it in certain terrain, because they were always too late or poorly adapted to the fierce competition and altered environment, until a balanced state of climax vegetation was reached.

While Valdez's selection as the Terminal site had at first been considered as incredible good fortune, it had been redefined by time to be Valdez's manifest destiny. At one of the stores, a gentle unhurried man of sixty told his own story of Good Friday 1964 as he closed up and counted the drawer of his 1906 brass cash register styled with bas relief Baroque cupids and arabesques. A Liberty ship in the harbor of the old town had broken anchor and been swept ashore, and then sent back to the bay unscathed by the tidal waves, although everyone at work on the docks perished. That same wave had come into this man's house, which he had just left after putting a pot of coffee on the stove. "When I got back afterward, the watermark was this high above the stove, but the coffeepot had floated out and drifted back to the same burner. First all was calm and regular, then fire broke out everywhere." The earthquake was equivalent to the energy released by fifty thousand Hiroshima atomic bombs. Its epicenter was only miles away, as Valdez sits on the very edge of the tectonic plate of a whole drifting continent.

He slammed the drawer shut and ran his left hand across the top of the register, erasing but little dust. "And this old money holder here from the store is the only other thing besides that coffeepot that I've still got from a solid home and a mature business, the only tie. You said it, it's really a beauty, I'd never sell it to a soul." A dull thud echoed through the room. The storekeeper, visibly shaken, looked at his watch and then relaxed. "Oh, it's six o'clock. Just them blasting again, telling all of us it's time to go home and eat dinner."

All of the mountains wavering above have their beginnings in the sea. A full school of islands, islets and ragged rocks runs rampant throughout Prince William Sound, like killer whales defending the three-thousand-foot-wide channel of Valdez Narrows between Middle Rock and Entrance Point. On maps, Prince William Sound has the shape of a liquid spilled in very ruptured terrain: all manner of ragged sorties into nooks, crannies and coves of the most creative configurations. One of the men who had worked with George Perkins on a marine ecology study in the bay worried about the navigation problems for the Very Large Crude Carriers soon to call for the oil. "Go down in September or in August and just watch the circus. Of course they will have pilots, but we had the most experienced one in the whole region, and we ran aground eighteen times. Just look at the shifting currents, tides, fog and rocks there and then wonder about the tankers. Someone will really screw Alyeska in the future. . . . We did a really good baseline study there — it was virgin, that is, a completely natural state, totally unaffected by the acts of man. But now Alyeska admits that five hundred gallons of crude a day minimum will be dumped into the bay from the ballast treatment facility even after 'state of the art' purification. What will happen after ten years of that? What will happen when the fog rolls in around the rocks?"

Supertankers are just huge versions of the eighteen storage tanks then under way, and the thirty-two total when two million barrels a day flow south from Prudhoe to the sea. Only the tankers are much larger, and they float and navigate the Narrows; the tanks do

nothing but sit and wait. A 250,000-deadweight-ton tanker doing sixteen knots takes at least three miles to stop in open seas. In fog and other conditions warranting slow speeds of four to five knots, a supertanker loses steerageway and tends to sheer off course unless helm and engines are artfully employed; the ship may become incapable of maneuvering. A 250,000 ton tanker is over a thousand feet long, the size of the Empire State building, and cannot turn in narrow passages, so it must rely on other vessels to avoid it. Two studies commissioned in 1976 by the state Pipeline coordinator's office predicted that about two million gallons of oil will be spilled as a result of a predicted six collisions, one explosion, six groundings, two rammings, four structural failures and one other accident listed as "all other." The studies did not take into consideration in any way the giant rock lying in the middle of Valdez Narrows, closing the passage to three thousand feet in width.

The drugstore in town, like most retail stores in Alaska, was a bookstore specializing in paperback westerns, best-sellers, and abundant Alaskana. Alaskans exercise their provincialism by reading more about themselves and their land than most any other group in the country, titles like "Growing the Giant Alaskan Cabbage," Cry in the Wilderness, "The ABC's of Prospecting Explained in Simple Everyday Language with Illustrations," Under the Aurora, "How to Pan Your Own Gold and Where to Seek It," in hardback and pamphlet. Only one copy remained of a new addition to Alaskana literature though, a book called Supership by Noel Mostert, about the other-worldly tankers that would be calling soon.

A shift change had taken place at the tank farm at six, and the twelve-hour night session was already half over. What darkness comes to Valdez in summer had arrived, darker than Fairbanks, which sees only twilight in July. The surveyors had been out all day getting stoned and seriously bird-watching with their transits as usual, at twenty-two dollars an hour since it was Sunday. The

crews had gotten together to compare notes and consult their bird guides while smoking some grass in one of the partially erected tanks with a couple of D-9 operators who had been playing their favorite game of stoned tag in the woods, madly crashing around anywhere in the huge cats.

Four of the surveyors began to enact a joyous scene under the Big Top, trained bears with thick collars performing on tops of barrels and leaping through hoops of steel festooned with fire or crepe, poking into old clown routines to improvise gags that nourished the trance. Lions in cages and lion tamers in gleaming knee-high boots radiant as pitch, clowns clanking cymbals and striking the tank's iron flanks with oversized mallets in mock anger. A plethora of fantastic scenes and improbable identities in one broad blur, while the others were alternately applauding kids buoyed by balloons, and responsible adults providing sober commentary. Someone grabbed a sledge and struck the rim of the rising tank repeatedly, like an enormous gong in an Asian city's marketplace alerting the populace to an impending imperial announcement. It muted everyone inside, the sound of a flawed bell ever so slightly miscast or a mess hall kitchen stew pot not designed for music, tone waves that overlap and strive to catch their predecessors. A penetrating, heaving sound that rushed out from its origin in shock waves, coming from a place so deep it felt like the glaciated mountains were breathing with an iron lung.

George and Joan and Randy sat for a moment in the deafening silence produced when the two roaring white gas cookstoves were shut off. Tea finally brewing, only the Alladin lamp lit, Amy and Eileen asleep in the quarter of the cabin designated as bedroom, individual raindrops picking out a polyphony on the roof. Another sound arrived, an unusual one as queer as the mad cry of the loon, as frightening as a foghorn warning at sea. Outside to see if a boat were near, they felt their eyes move away from the relaxed darkness, drawn across the bay to the Terminal site. A battery of generators droned all night there now and was audible at the cabin, where once there was stillness. There had always been only the Milky Way to guide nocturnal wanderings, but tonight huge light towers had appeared to glare upon the work site for the night shift cranes and blasters. As they watched the burning lights and creeping beacons growing right before them just across the dark blue bay suddenly far too small, the vague drone came once again, now clearly from the Terminal. It rolled in a fog across Port Valdez, an unearthly gathering Gregorian chant cast from steel.

Fair
Banks and Tender Ladies

Fairbanks is not a descriptive name. It was never meant to be. Fairbanks is a curious blend of arctic alchemy and Gay Nineties false fronts set in a random bend of the murky Chena River. Its honorary position as gateway to a distant colony's lush fields of wealth — once gold, now oil — and the vast wilds north of the Yukon is made all the more remarkable at first sight. The contorted glacial peaks one expects to surround Fairbanks aren't there. But the luxury of space pervades the town; it opens to the boreal forests and the places where men trade themselves for money. Fairbanks lacks settledness. It is a squatter colony of desperate wayfarers, missionaries and expatriated ascetics in the throes of those first faltering steps toward the ranges far beyond.

On First Avenue, not two blocks south of the sojourning Chena River, resides the U.S. Geological Survey map office for Alaska. It is a modest stuccoed structure, situated next to a barn-red frame house hosting geraniums barely able to contain themselves to their rusted troughs and buckets. There are other troubled frame buildings, alternately complaining of the heat or cold to senior log cabins nearby, surrounding galvanized trailers stuffed in alleyways amid pragmatic cinder block monoliths. The most illustrious structure and hotel in town is the Polaris Building, a six or seven story concrete lapse of imagination that passes for architecture. There is no real architecture in Alaska; the place is too fresh. It is hard and expensive to bother with anything but basic amenities. No public aesthetic exists, no collective quest for a sense of community. But a personalized beauty abounds in the network of hand-sculpted cabins tucked out of sight.

Fannie Mae McDaniel, the archetypal Sourdough woman, one part little warm-hearted schoolteacher with fawn-brown glasses to three parts rough-riding mountain lady — done it all and still ready to go — worked the counter at the USGS office. Requests by phone and in person were handled there for many of the most unlikely spots in an unpredictable state. But Fannie or someone else in the office always seemed to know the location well, from having actually been there or dreamed and plotted how. There were voluminous demands for maps of the area the Pipeline was to pass through, from sportsmen, workers and research specialists investigating one thing or another and curious wanderers and idle prospectors. Each pass and glacial tarn was talked about by the help at the counter in a soft, reverent tone that suggested a busy past of intimate collaboration with the Supreme Being.

Fannie and a girl friend were restless in New York after World War II, and set out on a round-the-world tour. Juneau was proposed as one of the first stops, but it proved to be the last. Fannie met a gold miner studying there, married him, and for a couple years lived in the wild Brooks Range on a small lake accessible only by plane and dogsled. She seldom left the state thereafter; there was no need to go anywhere else. "Oh, I guess you could say I've done my share here. . . . It's a Great Land, like the name's supposed to mean in the Aleut language, 'Alyeska' actually it is, and I've been all over it. It finally got too cold and hard in the Brooks and so my husband got a job down here in town working maintenance out at the airport. But even that's too much for his health, his legs bother him and he has smoking problems, so we broke down and made the big decision — to go to Phoenix this winter and probably stay there. Ohh, it's awful, I hate to even think about it . . . it's been so long and so good. But things are changing so much here it's just not the same, anyway. Like people like us say, used to be you could leave a hundred dollar bill on the counter in a bar and go to the restroom and not worry a minute that it'd be gone when you got back. It's true! And you used to know everybody who walked around town, say hello and all. It was just a matter of time before this Pipeline got going, I guess, so maybe leaving's not so bad. My husband always says to the younger folks, 'Don't ever grow old in Alaska, it's too hard. Stay young always!'" She disappeared into the sprawling labyrinth of metal shelving to locate a 1:250,000-scale map of the Skeklukshuk Range, wherever that may be.

The frontier shows through in Fairbanks. It eases its way out of the hills across the Chena River, north and east of town. That particular sluggish bend of a river en route to the baffling inconsistencies of the Yukon is one of the last spots to feel the push of a vast tract of tundra to the south: permafrost, bog, black spruce. North of Fairbanks even a few miles the topography grows intricate. There are only a few roads there, and all of them begin in town.

Every day in the first spring of the Pipeline back in '74, the map office was crammed with newcomers and old-timers trying to get in and get what they needed to get out of town. Anywhere — it didn't matter where one was headed, the idea was simply to be in motion. That's the way the state is, in its summer phase, bursting the grip of a winter that begins in September and lasts into May. The rowdy outgoing full-throttle insanity of the summers is matched in intensity by the introspection and psychic incest of the winters. Too much cold darkness breeds "cabin fever"; it gets to everyone.

The divorce rate in Alaska increases significantly in February and March. But this year especially the people were restless with inertia from the years of forecasting instant wealth, all the repetitive speculation promising *start-up any day now, really, I heard it from the business agent himself, no lie . . .*

Fairbanks is a dirty, seething town on the edge of Americana, but one stuffed with fine, diamond-core people who stay the hell away from each other as much as possible and do whatever they must in peace. A standard green highway sign on the Steese Highway, where it reluctantly comes out of the domes and birches to cross the Chena and resign itself to some time in town, stated the population as twenty-eight thousand and a handful or two. The numerals were crudely crossed out and replaced by the simple epithet: "Too many." By late 1974 too many was about sixty-three thousand. Downtown is a basic grid pattern fifteen streets to a side that boasts the services of a Mormon potato town of seven or ten thousand in southern Idaho.

And the whole top half of the state, an area 750 by 400 miles, the size of California, is outfitted, comforted and accosted here.

"Break-up," in the spring, when the iced-over rivers slowly loosen in the warmth and then break free with a rifle shot to crash to the sea, huge blocks of ice like surging glaciers; break-up usually brings motion and mud. In April and May the airports and highways were humming with a choreographed mass rush to see the summer solstice in Fairbanks on the twenty-first of June, when the sun dips in the north for a scant two hours and the Goldpanners or Glacier Pilots or another baseball squad begins a game at eleven P.M. With its easy money and honest-to-goodness wooden Gold Rush bars, for the first weeks Fairbanks became an intoxicatingly decadent overstuffed Victorian couch, delightful to sink into, hard to leave.

For the moment, the Pipeline was only a constant dissonance whirling in the background, an abstract idea on the planning tables. People did disappear from the hiring halls daily and each story of success in faking the one-year Alaskan residency requirement for Local Hire status — a provision hammered into the project agreement — was repeated to the point where it began to bifurcate over and again into a whole new set of related stories. Anything could be believed because nothing could be. The Pipeline was uniquely American in its promise, its innocence, and its greed. Nothing went unaffected; it swallowed everything like a galactic black hole. You could never neatly focus on anything or even describe what was there, the constant whirl of machinery just over the rise. The Pipeline is one of those last blinding flashes of recognition and salvation, in which a man could — in a very short, albeit tragically brutal and searing time, like a battle or gold-strike — erase the bitter, burning rage of a life of waiting and personal impotence, and transform his destiny.

Fairbanks is not much of a place to wait for anything. In 1974 the Bureau of Labor Statistics determined that the Anchorage consumer price index was 28 to 48 percent above Seattle; Fairbanks was 49 to 70 percent higher. To actually move in and settle down is reasonable, providing Alaskan wages for the extremes of the local economy. A cheeseburger goes for $2.25. The Fairbanks McDonald's is their third largest in volume in the world, following the franchise in West Germany and the one in Anchorage. Gasoline is seventy-six cents a gallon; and 90 percent of the state's food is imported. Everything comes from someplace else. A gas station mechanic repairing the inevitable part failures from the rough roads and weather gets twenty-one dollars an hour. Pizzas are about five bills, exclusive of extras. It costs a buck-forty just to get in a cab and close the door. From January 1974 to October 1975 Anchorage, let alone Fairbanks, experienced a 23.2 percent increase in cost of living. Since one of the lowest allowances is for Houston, the Texans who work in Alaska and spend their earnings at home in the classic colonial fashion do very well.

Stories and embellished rumor are the mainstay of any vanguard: there are few institutions and fewer rules in the frontier stages of a society, only an oral tradition firmly founded on bantering, hoodwinking, and seduction. Stories are judged only by the plausibility of the teller and the told, and allow ambiguous rephrasings that transform the teller into an actor in the myth. Everyone is an expert. There is a bright illusion of equality and fraternity in the early stages of a boom, like the first fresh glow of a revolution, when information and position are equally available or not. A boom is a return to a cheerful anarchy, a rejection of the lessons of a lifetime.

"Margarita – no glass"

Word was out. People streamed into the state by the Alaska Highway, which felt close to 49,000 vehicles lumber along it in '74 and 57,000 the following year, a 27 percent increase. A hotel room might easily go for thirty-eight dollars a night when available; entire floors or whole hotels were rented to subcontractors for their employees. The first spring of the boom saw 337 transients bedded down in the mission from mid-April to mid-May, and 1697 men exactly a year later in 1975. There were 186 rental units advertised in September 1974, and only eighteen available by the following March, before new units hastily built in response to the population pressures came into the market that summer. Average rents for two-bedroom apartments were $341 to $408 a month in late '74, and $448 to $525 a year later.

A blond freak from northern California hitched north for work, his dog giving birth to seven puppies on the backseat of a car while on the Alaska Highway, near Fort Nelson. He set up a canvas wall tent in the late fall snows and sub-zero temperatures until the crude oil-burning Yukon stove overzealously burned the rig to the ground. Their next home was beneath the University Avenue bridge over the Chena until the cold drove him to abandoned cars for protection from the wind. A lot of days got spent in libraries and laundromats. He got work as a day laborer, doing anything, and met Harve while they toiled carrying twenty-foot spruce cants — three-sided cabin logs — for a home on the edge of town. They took in a little bluegrass music out at the Howling Dog Saloon in Ester, and Harve offered to let him move into their abandoned gold mine. It was twenty-some miles out of town past Cleary ski area to Fairbanks Creek, and then a four-mile walk through the woods on snowshoes to the site. Derelict buildings and antiquated equipment filled the gulch that Harve and his wife and another couple occupied. Three of the four had part-time jobs in town, and daily snowshoed and drove and hauled water by backpack and sled four miles each way to keep the place running. One main room of the old cook shack was barricaded and sealed with plastic securely enough to keep out the bitter wind; wood was chopped by lantern each night after the long slog home in darkness.

The community held together well into winter, until Harve's eighteen-year-old wife contracted a bronchial infection and the two gave up to drive all the way home to Michigan. The others moved into town, sold the puppies, and started waiting for the union calls, every morning.

People stayed longer than they anticipated, imagining a quick transition to the Pipeline camps with their fresh linens, pastries, and all the free grade-B movies anyone could possibly absorb. Life at the mission could drift on and on. One man hitched up the Alcan, arrived with forty dollars after a two-week trip, and checked into the mission. The second night, the blond hitchhiker got rolled on Third Avenue by two winos and had his glasses smashed. There was no money to have them repaired, and his eyesight was too poor to get work. Waiting can be an insidious series of subtle double binds, an alienating limbo often visible in the stories eyes can tell.

Numerous families crowded their homes with a dozen patient workers at ten or twenty dollars a night, off to the union halls each morning and afternoon, then back to cook in the wife's kitchen, relax around the TV, and crash on the rec room floor. The kids just played around them; it was the money that mattered, maybe six hundred dollars a week. Plywood partitions were raised in one basement and the resulting cell-sized "rooms" rented for fifty dollars a week, or two hundred a month. They were thin membranes amplifying the explicit sounds next door. It was fun to monitor Butch's progress with the Mexican waitress he brought in a couple of times a week. The guys used to say that he was so ugly he couldn't have gotten anybody that wasn't shivering from the cold all the time like her. Mostly, no one cared.

A Hopi named Kee Whitesheep managed a lively rooming house, near the end of Second Avenue that meets the Chena River. It was owned by one of the newly created Native corporations, which purchased the place as an investment in the early stages of the

Dancers, Gold Rush Hotel

boom. Kee — classic American Indian features, sinewy and statuesque — had come up from the Southwest with his wife and five kids at the behest of his cronies there, all curious about both political events in Alaska and the Pipeline itself. After activist work with the American Indian Movement in the Southwest, Kee decided that he "wanted to see firsthand what happened to us at home eighty and a hundred years ago . . ." The string of treaties and breaches of promise that comprised the Hopi experience was seen as similar to the Alaska Native Claims Settlement Act of 1971 in its sweeping promise, so he wanted to watch progress and the political process.

After waiting in vain at the Electrical Workers Union for that high-paying Pipeline job, Kee visited several of the Native centers in town, and was offered management of this house. It did not pay as well as the union job, but did allow him to be with his family. And, to work with the Native movement as part of a new managerial class spawned by the broad investments the profit-making corporations made with ANCSA's seed money. Kee's not sure whether he'll stay in Alaska. He wrote back to his friends in the grazing country to tell them not to hasten to the North, and kept on collecting eighty-three dollars a week for a single room in the dorm. With communal bathroom. No one seems to be born in Alaska; people just decide they were meant for the place.

Second Avenue is the heartthrob of Fairbanks. Concentrated within two trying blocks are a fair percentage of the bars, brawls, and broads the town has to offer. There are a few exotic foreign restaurants, tourist gift shops full of jaded novelties and Mexican silk paintings of panting sled dogs and placid polar bears, and the Lacey Street Theatre with its neon Tlingit totem motifs announcing another cowboy or disaster film, half a year late. And Coop Drug, a sundry goods bonanza akin to Woolworth's, but crowded with visiting Eskimos from places known by such melodious names as Unalakleet or Mitliktavik, still in sewn skin parkas and pullover cotton *kuspuks* — fur-rimmed floral wind parkas — despite the reasonable temperatures inside. It's the nexus of social life for many of Fairbanks's five thousand Natives, and their visiting kin. The general decor of "Two Street," as it came to be known by Pipeliners, is high false fronts and an orderly array of nondescript boxes posing as buildings. A Hollywood set for a film about mining in Montana between the wars, the Civil and the First, that is, complete with cowboy, Indian, and mountain man extras.

A tousle haired, toreador panted Aleut woman hustled all night that first summer in the twilight that lasted and never left, only eighty miles south of the Arctic Circle. Bars stayed open until five A.M., then closed until seven-thirty to clean up and satisfy local ordinances. A Yellow Cab pulled up to the Flame Lounge and a sidewalk dialectic began, with the cabbie as interpreter between monied interest and the natural resource. The client was young and inexperienced, full of verbal fumblings punctuated by the rhythmic snapping of a shiny breast pocket button on his Levi's jacket. Finally the lady in question, made up in her best look of ruffled maternal know-how, shoved her hand in his right hip pocket and led him through the damaged, faded door past the proud moose trophy blinking in the dark and the incandescent electric pinball machine.

Fairbanks, like most boom towns, has had an illustrious history of hookers. The workers and G.I.s liked the Athapaskan women the best, for their relaxed nature and long, black-haired beauty. In early 1974 the House Judiciary Committee held hearings on the possible legalization of prostitution in Alaska, to keep it under control and deter organized crime. The topic comes up regularly, especially since the Native women were driven off the streets by competition from the black professionals from Chicago and Vegas, who arrived before the first fall of Pipeline work.

The initial week of March of '74 was lucrative for a twenty-eight-year-old woman from Outside. She purchased tickets to fly into Deadhorse, a construction

camp just south of Prudhoe Bay on the North Slope, to sell magazine subscriptions, and stayed five days "before they finally shipped me out of there," along with her take of $5300. The cost for services ran between $75 and $500. She checked into a hospital for fatigue immediately upon her forced return to town. By a week later, she had already spent all but about $500.

Five women — "some of them so ugly it was like having your eyes poked out" — in a Winnebago camper from Miami, with two husky Italian drivers in dark sunglasses, arrived in Fairbanks in June and stayed in a campground for several weeks before departing for the work camps. Their outing had been organized in Florida, apparently one of a number of similar groups dispatched to various ripe territories throughout the states. This quintet decided to try the Pipeline, drove north to cross the Yukon River by boat, and canvassed Five Mile Camp briefly before they were thwarted by the authorities. Later in the summer, the Winnebago turned up in Valdez. One of the women made the mistake of propositioning the city manager; they were off again up the Richardson Highway, stopping in towns and Pipe camps along the way.

The "Paradise Dating Service . . . Operated BY Pipeliners, FOR Pipeliners," according to a leaflet distributed at the airport to incoming passengers disembarking from Pipeline flights, offered "the prettiest girls available in Fairbanks" for a hundred dollars an hour. "Dates" could be arranged by calling a telephone number in town, and leaving an address, a time, and "preference of BLONDE, BRUNETTE, or REDHEAD." Paradise was licensed by the State Department of Revenue, and had applied for a certificate of registration for sales and service tax from the Fairbanks North Star Borough.

The Flame Lounge and the French Quarter are the town's two most prominent entertainment spots. They sit almost back-to-back on First and Second avenues, barely separated by alleys busy day and night with all sorts of passion plays, desperate last standoffs, and low tide conviviality. Eighty percent of the prostitution arrests up to November 1975 were made in or near the two bars, according to the New York *Times*. In the fall of '75 the *All-Alaska Weekly* ran headlines stating that "Fairbanks Becomes Wild City . . . Prostitution up 5000 Percent." On a Friday night in September there were a hundred persons in the Flame; twenty-one were known prostitutes. With its bikinied dancers, stylish pimp and prostitute scene — considered at least as entertaining as any of the proffered acts themselves — and general enthusiastic go-to-hell decadence, the Flame was de rigueur for anyone just back from the Slope with a roll of hundreds. It suffered its own Pipeline impacts of a sort, as the bouncers and barmaids were interviewed by CBS, NBC, the Washington *Post*, the New York *Times*, German and Japanese video crews, the BBC, the Seattle *Times, Newsweek, Time,* and everybody else who came through town.

"There's no bullshit left after McGrath. It usually takes about that long for the others to drop out of the race" — the Iditarod, a thousand-mile dogsled race from Anchorage to Nome — "and after McGrath it's just all really fine people doing something they like to do." Richard, a bush pilot just in from Nome, well over four hundred miles away, greased fifties hair drawn straight back over a majestic crown, and silver aviator glasses; Richard eased his solid frame back in the molded plastic chair, fragile by comparison. "No, drugstore cowboys like back in Colorado don't make it up here, 'cept maybe down in Palmer. It's the 'mountain man' here, I guess, whatever you want to call it, Buck folding knife and all, a guy who knows how to get around the country okay and keep himself in one piece, and in a good head. Fix the truck, stoke the sauna, all that . . ." The Pastime was getting crowded, so Richard moved to a stool by the counter with the smooth skeletal efficiency bred by a life in the woods.

The woman behind the counter smiled at him, and at the perennially more bizarre array of customers, virtual caricatures, she thought — *c'mon you guys, you've got to*

Masseuses, Thee Body Shop, Anchorage

be kidding. She had anthracite-black hair too well taken care of for a waitress, and wore a tight body shirt with Great Gatsby twenties motifs, ironic beneath the "Chili $1.50" scrawled in black and red on brown cardboard. Her quick-to-come yet cautious smile and experienced air said "dancer."

Eirene, a name no one could ever quite pronounce, was an ex-dancer for the Flame, recruited and sent North by her new agent back in Boise for an eight-week run. A proud raven of a woman of Greek extraction, too frail for Fairbanks's unrelenting cold, Eirene got off the plane with her fine-haired golden retriever at minus-twenty one day in mid-October. Her shoestring budget was fashioned around her agent's urgent exhortations of "'a hundred dollars a day in tips, the boys are just rolling in the stuff when they come off the Line, no, really! and they just need Women and Legs and lust for anything that fits the description, just laying down the tens and twenties like nothing just to *see* you dance, nothing more. . . . Go or you're a fool . . .' I never should have fell for it." She signed and caught the next flight north.

In a tight Boise job market and the encroaching boredom of a static professional life, the Flame sounded fine, at least full of potential, maybe a little too good. Eirene danced for four nights, rowdy G.I.s and Pipeliners trying to pump fistfulls of dollars into her black satin bikini bottoms, dancing on tabletops for an extra tip just inches from the gold teeth and toothpicks and mesmerized eyes, to a jukebox jammed full of quarters, never stopping all night.

But life in the dancers' trailer complex was nice because of the sisterly affection and support it offered. "Well, we're all in this together, so it's been good to feel so close to all the girls. They're all very beautiful people, really, and we take care of each other, brush each other's hair, relax and just *be*. It's not what everybody thinks. And it *is* six hundred a month, not much for up here, but enough for now. The Flame can't last for me, too many hungry men and too much male energy all wound up in one spot, so I think I'll probably do the Eielson officers' club gig for a while; it's no hassles. But maybe this thing down in Paxson I was talking about will work out with the union. It goes like this: I'm trying to get official Native status as it'll be a lot easier to get on the Pipeline, almost surefire being a woman, too. I've got this friend there, and he thinks that it can be set up okay with the union people, I'm so dark that it should be easy to pass for a Tlingit . . . just have to keep myself together until it works out." She brought breakfast orders to two cabbies; it was 3:45 A.M.

"The Flame thing never could've worked. I like to dress up in nice clothes and feel attractive to men, to be a professional dancer — it's a profession, you know — but not to raise expectations." She had always felt both vulnerable and able to control men with her sexuality, and was caught in some curious paradox of innocence and arrogant decadence. "I'm staying on here because of the incredibly favorable odds — there are a whole lot of well-off handsome bachelors here. It's a good place for a woman, mighty fine. . . . But I'm kind of busy this week, Richard. Ah, maybe later, okay?"

There was a sudden commotion in the corner, one more insane drunken soliloquy on a well-worked theme. "I'm an FBI agent, FBI man, so I'm going to arrest you now! And this is true! And I'm telling you, one full-blooded or any-blooded Indian is worth three" — fingers form the digital equivalent and wave it high — "white men! And that's all I know!" He made a stumbling exit almost literally through the glass door, and everyone went back to eating.

Dancer, PJ's, Anchorage

Martin and Bonnie live in a sixteen-by-sixteen-foot log cabin some seven miles out in Goldstream valley, an unbelievably rich ore site now reduced to a haven for relaxed students of snowflakes. Fairbanks is known for its cabin culture centering around the University of Alaska community, and its extreme winter weather. Martin is a blaster and teaches the art to union classes; his wife Bonnie is a union member taking the course. They've done well by the union and now bring in a sizable sum between them. It's given them stable income in a town and state with unemployment figures traditionally around a third of the labor force, due to highly seasonal jobs and laggard growth. The low ceiling of the cabin is entirely covered with rejection slips from magazines of every description pinned there by the former occupant, a writer who never quite blossomed. But they live in relative ease, drinking out of paper cups "provided courtesy of Alyeska," eating steaks from the dining hall and whatever else can be rounded up and smuggled home. Bonnie now vacuums the tiny cabin regularly to keep it clean, while listening to the recent country-rock records on their stereo and mammoth Bose speakers, the largest and latest available. It's a bit like wearing earphones.

Following the big strike at Prudhoe in 1968, the find that started North Slope development and the building of the Pipeline, a consortium of oil companies was organized to fund and manage the massive project. In June of 1969, an unincorporated joint venture of the three major lease holders, Atlantic Richfield, British Petroleum, and Humble Oil, made application to the Department of Interior for permission to build a hot-oil pipeline along an eight-hundred-mile route through the public domain down to Valdez. The company was called the Trans Alaska Pipeline System (TAPS), and it expected to get permission within a month from then Secretary of Interior Walter Hickel, the evangelical, well-known Alaskan developer and politician. As it turned out, consent was not granted for five years of hard-nosed questioning and battling in the courts.

TAPS began hiring every available well-connected newspaperman, academic, and politician in the state, and at the local level in towns heavily impacted. A certain explicit chauvinism was in the air, a feeling that here was a project that could free the nation from domination by foreign powers; a glorious adventure of empire on the vastest scale imaginable, like the recurrent fantasy of a road to Nome, or the incredible Ramparts Dam scheme, a five-million-kilowatt project that would have produced the largest artificial lake in the world and generated several times more energy than the state's entire current and anticipated consumption. The Ramparts Dam was a full dress rehearsal for the Pipeline debate and logic of development, down to the special interest groups, participants, shadowy maneuvers behind the scenes in Washington, and the immensity of the concept; the fight over the project raged nationally from 1959 to 1967. The Prudhoe strike occurred the following year. And now it was the proposed Susitna Dams in Devil's Canyon; just the sort of grand idea that tickled Alaskans in some dark corner of their expansive souls. In the case of TAPS, not so much increased accessibility to the wilds as sheer audacity was the key to acceptance and respect. Paradoxical, this collective arrogance about a land so treasured in all its many manifestations, but Alaskans contain multitudes. They love both the splendid expanses, and the mammoth schemes of men to change the land unalterably.

Then the September tenth oil and gas lease sale on 430,000 acres around Prudhoe Bay was held and $900,041,605.34 was collected by the state auctioneers on that one day. Certified checks for 20 percent of the total were whisked to a waiting plane and immediately deposited in banks in California, to collect the substantial interest. Meanwhile, back in foggy, jubilant Juneau, the state began to conjure up plans for its windfall. The Pipeline had arrived as an idea, with Alyeska (the name TAPS thoughtfully discarded) billed as a paternal savior promising a new life — and a job — to all.

It was an important night, an evening of confrontation between two of the state's major figures in politics and business, an exercise in power extraordinaire. The debate had been properly built up into the remarkable event it just might be, via full-page advertisements in both Thursday's and Friday's Fairbanks *News-Miner*, an acre of print and pronouncements strewn around town. Jesse Carr, secretary-treasurer and unchallenged warlord of the Alaskan Teamsters, was to joust with Alyeska's president, Edward L. Patton, over the issue of Tuesday's Alyeska clerical workers election for a bargaining representative and a place in one of the unions. Patton didn't show, and only the mute wife of the opposing Laborers Union boss was present, so the show belonged to Jesse Carr.

"I wanted to challenge Mr. Patton face to face on this question, to go to you the people concerned with this election and just how you're paid for your services, but Patton didn't accept the invitation; he didn't come by so we could ask him questions directly and demand some direct replies. Well, I don't know, it's difficult to do collective bargaining when the employer doesn't show up at the table. I want to get Patton across the table from me on this one; I've waited a long time for a chance to sit across from him when things were balanced in our favor; yes, it's been pretty hard in the past, but now we've got him and I'm ready and delighted for the chance. Yes, delighted!" There is a trance generated by the simple pleas and exhortations, a highly pitched and sustained whine like that of a diesel rig pulling pipe up a long, slow hill in Atigun Pass.

There is no doubt that Jesse Carr is a man not simply for the people but unalterably of them, a man who stepped into life without fanfare or the inherent promise of the wellborn. He came quickly from the bottom where he mastered the rhetoric of power, polishing his techniques while ever refining his aims and ideals, learning what his people desired, until it crystallized into his slogan: "A fair day's wage for a fair day's work and freedom from foreseeable disaster for every Teamster and his family."

The ascent has left him impenetrably tough. He sits now near the podium, his hulking jaw and broad brow upholstered with skin callous and rhinocerine. But there are scars on that skin, visible as he fidgets with a paper without seeing the words written there, toils with the inner workings of an event and an empire. The scars glow pink in flame around their freshly healed edges when the action heats up again, whenever Jesse recalls memories of battles past as he awaits the return to the fray.

Jesse has always immersed his energies in the quick of any available conflict. Football and tennis in a high school outside of Los Angeles, fighting with the marines in the South Pacific, then north to the wild potential of Alaska in the restless, open years after the war, when everyone was on the road. First in 1949 for a visit, then again in 1950 for good. Jesse was a truck driver for the first year, later a business agent for the union, and for himself. Five independent unions were floundering until Jesse began to consolidate them into a single impressive Local 959, one that now brandishes 25,000 members from trucking, government, the Anchorage Police Department, and offices, and comprises a full 14 percent of the Alaskan labor force.

Because of the short Alaska construction season, Carr has a headlock on the Pipeline and most other projects in the state. He has boasted that "I've got the hammer to shut it down," and the several walkouts — in the form of prolonged "safety meetings" — have effectively demonstrated that Carr is one of the two or three most powerful men in the state. The Teamster pension, one of five funds of the local, will soon pass $100 million, as it grows by a million dollars a week. A Teamster trucker earns $11.13 an hour, with another $3 paid by the employer directly to the union for the pension fund. Carr was indicted in 1968 and 1969 on a total of six felony offenses ranging from extortion to embezzlement, but all of the cases were dropped before trial: four for lack of evidence, two because the principal witness had to undergo "extensive medical treatment" and was in "no physical condition to testify at trial." The Teamsters are one of the state's biggest landlords, are building a $15 million hospital and a $5 million professional clinic next to the $7 million headquarters mall building which was dedicated in the fall of 1974;

Jesse Carr

another $6.5 million complex is under consideration in Fairbanks.

Jesse, a member of the board of directors of one of the state's major financial institutions, the National Bank of Alaska, has two favorite sayings that summarize his philosophy: "Power is like being a lady — if you have to tell them you are, you ain't." In practice, it usually goes with a rejoinder inscribed in a brass plaque in his office: "When you've got them by the balls, their hearts and minds will follow."

"And if I'm not right about this, let me promise you here and now that I'll jump from the top of the Northward Building to the concrete below, head first into the pavement." The crowd is pleased. Even if the session doesn't answer their questions, it's been entertaining. Politics in Alaska has traditionally been based more on personal character then political ideology or partisanship. But the ebullience breeds faith and converts; no one leaves the hall, few squirm on the folding chairs. He could easily be selling bottled elixirs from a soapbox or wagon, or soliciting votes as a whistle-stop politician of the prairies. Honesty and enthusiasm exude from Carr. The typists are not simply taking dictation now or reproducing the words of others; they are here on their own, actors in a poignant drama.

Three of his lieutenants flank Carr on the speakers platform, advance men and interceptors for him, screening and emphasizing and handling the tough ones. Their taste in ties and trousers hints at the easily recognized accents and predictable rhetoric that they use to clarify points and raise questions. The chunky guy with the pale blue plaid trousers, different plaid sport coat and flashy tie — and a thin white belt supposed to hold all of these pieces together — rises to relate a story the Teamsters emcee thought was the appropriate reply to a question from the floor. He smiles professionally and does his part, glances expectantly at the authorities to see if it went well, finds approval, and sits down again.

At one point Jesse asks for a word from a neo-Teamster who had previously opposed conversion to union bargaining. "George, where's George? George can tell you best about the benefits of the union. George wasn't convinced at first, but he finally decided to go along with us. Come on up, George." George's enthusiastic testimony would have fit nicely in that huge evangelist tent down in the Tanana Valley Fairgrounds last summer, the one set up for the "Operation Frontier" Pipeline preaching campaign that drew spokesmen for the faith from all through the South. So be it, brother, Jesse Carr is the Way out of manipulation by Alyeska; vote Teamsters on Tuesday, ladies, and your typing shall be properly rewarded . . .

Afterwards the crowd mills about to chat with the Teamsters stalwarts planted throughout the audience. Most of the group of eighty or so are younger women, curious about the election and filled with the gossip and indecision that uncertain choices generate. Women, women in baby blue toreador pants and tops with matching eyeshadow; in the blue jeans, down parkas and heavy Canadian Sorrel boots — felt-lined and considered indispensable here — that mark cabin dwellers and cross-country ski buffs; black women in platform heels and body shirts, all present at a Teamsters meeting in one of the smartest rooms in town, at the Travellers Inn. One can't help but think back to the women's movement poster so often seen of Golda Meir, and its apt caption: "But can she type?"

Alyeska Pipeline Service Company has a completely unabashed adherence to the animated wonder of giant, brooding industry and the marvels it has wrought. There's a glint of the vigorous faith in machines and ideas translated into steel of Russian Reconstructionism, in the period between the wars. Alyeska is thrilled by the image of itself: it's an archetypal Alaskan adventure in forcing a stylish dream into reality, from an undifferentiated vastness little meddled with before. Alyeska is enthralled with the telling of a rousing good yarn in distant, exotic lands, a slave to its own situation and deeds. Its public relations department sounds at best like Kipling on the British in India, though without all the fun; less some of the mystery. But like most autobiographers who begin the task too early in life, the self-consciousness generated by their careful eye toward history and the legend of themselves finally hamstrings the ballad itself.

"We'll be coming out into the studio in forty-five seconds."

"Stand by for slate. Slate is up!"

"KUAC-TV 'TVCC Alyeska'" is the title chalked on the slate. The local community college was making a video tape of a course offered for credit on the Pipeline, and given entirely by the public relations department of Alyeska. Larry Carpenter, a former member of the journalism department here at the University of Alaska, is being his affable self with the patient audience of about twenty students, a smiling liege preparing his fiefdom for the appearance of the lord: Edward L. Patton, Chairman and Chief Executive Officer of Alyeska.

"We've given Patton a lot of very difficult jobs, and one of those will be escorting President Ford around the Pipeline on Saturday. With Ford's history of tripping over things, I can see Ford tripping over a VSM or something out on the Line," Carpenter intoned like soothing, effervescent PR men are supposed to, to loosen up the formal atmosphere.

"Better than playing golf with Agnew, anyway . . ." added Patton as a literal aside, still in the aisle awaiting introduction. The comment slipped out of his mouth without its ever opening. Yet it was Agnew, as Vice President, who was presiding in the Senate on July 17, 1973, and cast the final tie-breaking vote to pass the Gravel Amendment and authorize the Alaska Pipeline.

Edward Patton's mouth is usually turned fully upside down in an inverted horseshoe, the simple arched line a youngster portraying sadness might draw. A ruffled wave of senatorial-silver hair, its thousand curly tendrils both boyishly cute and suspended in some grasping, indefinite threat, like Hokusai's print "Great Wave Off Kanagawa." Brown horn-rimmed glasses, canary shirt without buttons on the collar, and a rich Masters-green sport coat fresco the form of the man.

Somehow Patton seems ill at ease in his hardwood and soft light office in Anchorage. He has all the moves of a desert fox who needs room to deploy his impressive array of tricks. See him commanding tank trucks in polar deserts; playing big-time blackjack in Monte Carlo. The office is a staid blend of mahogany, dust, and plastic binders that lends the requisite air of solid reliability and technical competence. There is a well-positioned set of props for his authoritative job role: a reference work on *Permafrost,* a hernia's worth of legal volumes liberally scattered through progress reports and binding devices of all variety, and a slick, protective secretary. A four-foot-tall pair of scissors leans surreally against a cupboard covered in plaques and commendations from the reigning powers in Washington and Alaska. Otherwise, it's strictly modern business decor — no elegant originals by the masters, no especially fine taste or individual choice, only the official smiling Rotarian sobriety and Pipeline aerial photographs devoid of workers.

The cameras pressed in closer to try to pierce the lacquer of Patton's appearance. There were a few technical problems at first, more tuning and adjustment of the sound system to adequately capture the rich intonations and fibrous litany of a chairman's interplay with his always attentive aides. Patton talks with a mouth full

Edward L. Patton

of barnacled clams and crisp sand dollars from the San Juan beaches he's apt to visit in spare time, when not sailing his twenty-six-foot sloop in Washington State. Low decibel, gravelly, and slipped sleekly out of inanimate lips, a submarine voice well tailored to cryptic asides and off-the-record rebuttals.

Seaside Newport News, Virginia, was his hometown as a boy, before graduating from Georgia Tech in 1938 with a B.S. degree in Chemical Engineering. He joined an Exxon affiliate in Baton Rouge, Louisiana, the same year and served in the navy as commanding officer of several antisubmarine and escort vessels from 1941 to 1946. Back in Baton Rouge with Exxon, he progressed through a number of management positions before transferring to the Norwegian affiliate for the construction of a refinery, eventually returning to the United States in 1964, an adviser for Exxon operations in the Mediterranean, Middle East and the Far East. Just prior to coming to Alyeska, Patton managed the construction and operation of a major new refinery complex in Benicia, near San Francisco. It was there that he first came under and countered fire of environmental activists.

"The Sierra Club was a whole different group in the '66 refinery work, and I'd have to say that at about that time, oil industry/environmental relations entered a new period of an atmosphere of decreased sincerity. It was an era of campus riots and all that. . . . So, I'm not sure that my previous experience with environmental opposition was of any real assistance in this job, because of the very different nature of relations after about '66. . . . So much is emotional that I don't think I learned much from all that . . ." the veteran confided to a community college student between takes.

There are eight members of the Alyeska consortium, initially united in a complex formula: Sohio Pipe Line Company (33.34%), BP Pipelines Inc. (15.84%), ARCO Pipe Line Co. (21%), Exxon Pipeline Co. (20%), Mobil Alaska Pipeline Co. (5%), Union Alaska Pipeline Co. (1.66%), Phillips Petroleum Co. (1.66%), Amerada Hess Corp. (1.5%). Establishing the independence of Alyeska from its parent companies and increasing its influence in the federal government was Patton's primary work, at first. He eventually "began to get a

vision of the need for a Native claims act of Congress" as the only efficient way of settling the question and getting construction under way, "though the owners were of the opinion that it was not necessary." Patton went to Washington to inform Congress of the need; "That maneuver was successful." Then in 1973 "the Arabs were beginning to raise the price of oil so that got Congress's attention. . . . The turning point was July 17, '73 in my opinion, when Agnew voted to break the tie in the Senate and pass the Gravel Amendment. . . . They continued to do what I call dibble and dabble until the Arab-Israeli War broke out and the Arabs raised prices" in retaliation for U.S. aid to Israel, leading to a fast bill and Nixon's signature. "The final thing that stood in the way was the project agreement," signed on the twenty-third of January, 1974. "The largest private project in the past was the Disney World project. . . . Disney refused to begin until an agreement was signed, and their experience showed the value of a project agreement, which included a no-strike clause . . . compulsory arbitration of jurisdictional disputes . . . and unlimited prefabrication.

"As to highlights of the project, in addition to the congressional vote I'd have to point to the Arab Embargo. . . . One of the greatest things we've done was to place the order for the pipe in 1969, estimated to be four times as much now. . . . We can't say how much the cost of the whole thing has escalated as we don't have a bill of materials needed then, and the design has changed so much . . . I would have to guess we've designed this project three times over" due to unforeseen circumstances, incredible outright blunders, and environmental stipulations. The original project estimate was $900 million. Charles Elder, executive vice president of Alyeska, has sighed, "I really wish it would go away. It was never a very realistic estimate." A hundred million dollars was allocated right away for purchase of the steel pipe from Japan, the principal source of colonial investments in Alaska; hence, the remaining estimated $800 million has exploded to over $7 billion, perhaps to go as high as $10 billion.

Patton, dignified, casual, and obviously a man of the world, fields questions with enviable ease, as if he could

casually level and play it all-cards-out-on-the-table with a furtive sheikh or an epauletted African general. He's the kind of guy you might dream of for a boss — centered and his own man, no printout or speaker system voice for some vague, bureaucratic electromagnetic source; accessible, not the egocentric titan one might suppose. Feels like you could talk straight with the guy in the local beer joint around the corner. Only he'd still be winning somehow, every round.

"As to accidents, we're below the national average in construction and industrial production both." But all of the constant truck accidents and deaths on the Haul Road, "all the common carriers are not our baby, the ones that the Teamsters scream about," and so the official Alyeska figures conveniently don't reflect any deaths among its hundreds of subcontractors. The actual human toll is frightening. Everyone talks of the guys hauled off the workpad and put on the next plane south, strapped in upright position; the latest Teamster driver deaths on the "Kamikaze Trail," the Elliot Highway meandering from Fairbanks to the Yukon, along which three eighty-foot pipe sections at a time were driven, sixty thousand pounds of green steel. According to a New York *Times* story, the Bechtel Corporation, a principal contractor on the project, entered the relevant data into a computer after the first year, and was sobered by the printout: 273 of its own employees alone would die by the time the Pipeline was finished. A lot of them are dead already.

One major piece of advice Edward Patton has for other super projects is to carefully plan for all contingencies and possible variables, to exercise clairvoyance and *see* all that is to come. "This is particularly important in an underdeveloped area like Alaska, where you have to pull yourself up by the bootstraps to get anything done. . . . I don't expect in the life of the Pipeline that there will be a major oil leak. There will be small leaks, but that's not what you want to talk about. . . . The biggest environmental factor and impact may be the Valdez ballast facilities, so sophisticated that it was necessary to generate five times more power to run the facilities. That introduces more thermal and air pollution, certainly, in order to cut down on the amount of used ballast pumped into the harbor, quite a trade-off."

Larry Carpenter performed perfectly as the company's exuberant PR man with his ever-ready smile capped by a clipped mustache and bald cranium, the verbal juggler who effectively soothed irritated members of the community and press. Anything to help them forget or ignore the bitter bite of hard questions they'd mutter if they could, the ones that pilfer sleep at night and drive rigs into the ditch on icy mornings after.

"I'm always amazed at the sound of my own voice," Patton confided as he listened in the sound booth to the tape just made. He gracefully removed a thin fourteen carat gold pen from his suit pocket to add his signature to a document placed before him. After a quick survey of its meaning, Edward Patton strided with the refinement of oil ambassadors to a glass-topped table nearby, twice slowly wiped clear the dust with the heel of his left hand, and signed. The gold digital watch indicated it was time to head off to the airport for the late flight back to Anchorage, so he mechanically replaced the slim pen next to a tiny pocket slide rule. "Yes, it's always funny to hear your own voice . . ." he added to the young audio technician. He responded to one final query from the few students gathered at the back of the studio. "I don't think the people of Alaska will really know that the Pipeline is there, except as a major tourist attraction . . ."

"In KIAK Pipeline Country, it's 9:27 . . ." Peter Van Nort flicked a couple of switches inside the broadcasting studio, spun quickly to check the console behind him, and shot a preparatory smile at someone waiting patiently beside the vacant receptionist's desk. The sound-proofed door opened just long enough for the first line — "This house runs on sunshine, peace, and love" — of a song's chorus and all two hundred and twenty pounds of Peter Van Nort to slip out into the lobby.

A rustic hand-carved plaque right by the front door confirmed the location: "KIAK Big Country Radio . . . Dial 970 Fairbanks Alaska." A small Cessna airplane with floats in the upper left-hand corner mystically made its way through a dense cloud-bank of dark gnarls and knots, the wood's rich texture suggesting another epic northern saga already under way. Beneath the inscription sat a small log cabin, four scraggly black spruce growing out of the sod roof. The right border of the sign was defined by the tall latticework of an oil derrick that had its foundation near the cabin, but reached all the way into the clouds.

Pete chatted with the visitor for a while in his own initially intense but gradually warming way. The conversation was broken regularly by swift strides to one clipboard or printout or another, as Pete performed his duties.

A visitor brought a four-track demo tape to the station to see if it could get some air time. The song was called "Alaska Soul," sung by Jerry Mac, and written by "Yukon" Mike Dunham. They went into an empty studio and played the tape through a couple of times, and spoke of other country-western efforts to make Pipeline music. There was that Earl Shepard tune, Pete recalled, out on Charter Records, "I think it was called 'Black Gold' . . . of course Shepard has probably never been up to Alaska, so it wasn't much." The official Alyeska employee paper, *The Campfollower*, a down-home collection of news articles, and stories of workers jousting with enraged caribou and inventing outlandish recipes for the official Pipeline Polly drink, was the focal point of a constant barrage of poetry and songs in the best Alaskan tradition: heavy on the rhyming, light on

ideas. Edwin Knapp of Chandalar sent in his original composition, without the music.

Long White Winters

There's oil up there in that frozen north
No man really knows how much it's worth
But there's jobs up there and we need the dough
So we hit the trail of the Eskimo . . .

Well we came back from that far-off land
With a lot of dough and a great big plan
To buy a home and settle down
On a country lane near a little town

She was standing there when the plane flew in
Her eyes were bright and she wore a grin
I thought of the nights she had spent alone
While I labored hard in that frozen zone . . .

Pete Van Nort had seen plenty of them, but "Alaska Soul" was special and smelled and tasted authentic, heartfelt. He backed up against a wall of glossy eight-by-ten promo photos of Nashville aristocracy. Jerry Naylor's portrait was crisscrossed by an epitaph: "To ALL my friends at KIAK — How can I thank you enough!!" Charlie Pride was there in color, his face modestly cut off at the nose by a slick black and white shot of a young upstart recently on tour in Alaska. Peter tucked his pin-striped shirt into his new Wrangler jeans and promised to try and push Jerry Mac and Mike Dunham's tape.

I am an Alaskan, and I've known the northland all my life,
Her mountains were my mother's knee, her rivers were my
*   only wife.*
The two of us were just like one until the strangers came.
Alaska! Alaska! You'll never be the same.

My family left Southeastern with the totem poles, the fish and
*   rain*
Settled on the Tanana and tried to work a homestead claim.
Dad swore that he would beat the land, but I guess he beat
*   himself;*
When he couldn't prove it up, they gave it to someone else.

So we tried the trapping life, from Eagle to the Koyukuk,
Then to the Talkeetnas where we ran out of our mining luck.
My father froze out on the trail, and Mom burned with our
  store.
I hated you, Alaska! But I loved you even more.

Past my cabin north of Tok one day the foreign license plates
Came up the road like marching ants; they'd come to seal
  Alaska's fate.
I took a trip to Fairbanks, and it looked just like a war.
Alaska! Alaska! You don't know me any more.

I heard about the Pipeline, but I didn't really think it'd start.
Now the new folks fill the land. Oh God! It's tearing me
  apart!
They don't smile at you on the street, you can't hear no one
  sing.
Alaska! Alaska! To them you're just a thing.

I see the drunken Native now, and know why he thinks
  drinking's fun,
'Cause booze sure helps to blind your eyes to what the white
  man's greed has done.
I'm going to Second Avenue, get drunk, forget the pain . . .
Alaska! Alaska! Oh, why'd they make you change?

All five thousand watts of KIAK Radio came up to Fairbanks from a parent station in Anchorage in anticipation of the swelling Pipeline boom. The Alaska Native Claims Settlement Act had been signed by President Nixon in December 1971 and opened the possibility of actual work on the long-delayed project. Exactly nine months later on September 18, KIAK went on the air from six A.M. to midnight with the first country-western music in town. It was at a time when rock music was beginning to wane in popularity, and the pulsing truck-driving rhythms of C&W came back to life. It's music to run through the gears by, to drink beer and worry about the little woman back home and do all the things a migrant labor force must do. Good-humored hassles with the sheriff, brawls over favorite waitresses and their favors, machines out of control, vigilante squads against the local hippies, and indulgences in unabashed sentimentality: country-western was acomin' to town, with KIAK as its spokesman. It

was long overdue, for Alaska is a land that still worships heroes out in the open. It is two decades estranged from mainstream American life, and does all in its tenacious power to stay that way, serenading bush pilots, dog mushers and wolves.

After dashing into the "jock's" glass studio to make an announcement or two, Pete threw the system on automatic, and let the Schafer 902 Switch Memory begin the tapes. The Schafer Control Unit Model 901 is a particularly efficient device designed to produce a smooth, homogeneous and "professional" sound in radio via automation and pre-packaged broadcasts. There were only four such units in Alaska when KIAK went automatic, including KCAM in Glennallen on the Richardson Highway, halfway to Valdez, and KHAR-AM/FM, KNIK-FM, and KGOT-FM in Anchorage.

The management at KIAK wanted to lose the small town idiosyncratic flavor of the station and its hugely different jocks. You always wonder what they look like and try to piece their features together, boisterous extroverts and opinion makers. The individual jocks involved are not without second thoughts, for the Schafer system gradually eliminates them and vastly curtails their participation in air time, although it also provides some compensatory prestige for the station. Where there were five jocks spinning discs each twenty-four-hour day, there are now three. Most of their time goes into programming and preparation of "spots," commercial messages for advertisers. And talking a lot to themselves.

The Schafer main console has a digital time readout to the second in electric-beet colored numerals. There are four Revox A 77 Stereo reel-to-reel tape recorders on the right, which click into action with Prussian punctuality, a snapping of switches and engaging gears instead of the usual flurry of a jock's glottal stops and wheezes.

On the left are two Instacart bins of forty-eight cassettes each, all the spots and "promos" and PSA's necessary for a show: "Gold Hill Liquor," "Mukluk Shop," "Arctic First Federal Savings," "Pipeline of the North, and Petroleum Digest," "Aurora Motors." Address: 0487, Source: 14, Spot: 48, a panel with indicator lights and letters to let you know just where you are, all the time. A tape bank with the station identification and the time is prepared for every half-minute of the day and night, odd minutes on one tape on top, with the evens tape beneath it. They were all taped by the main system announcer in Los Angeles — "he's probably making a hundred thousand dollars a year for that" — and shipped north to KIAK and all the dozens of other stations around the country that subscribe to the system.

"It's pretty hard on the ego, frankly, kind of bruises you a bit, you know, but hopefully we can put our creativity and personality into the commercial spots instead. Actually, it's hard to get good jocks in Alaska these days anyhow, which is part of the reason for going to the Schafer system. This was an effect of the Pipe, as good radio people went up there to work as laborers or operators and earn three times as much money. KFRB, just across the way there, went through two different people last summer, who worked two months and then went on their way to the Slope. You know, the old 'Just send my cash and license up after me, fellas. . . .' Those two guys were staying in a Pipe flophouse, some grungy basement for eighty bucks a week, couldn't find anything else, and working a jock's hours, waiting to get on the Line.

"But I don't think that KIAK would bring country radio up here for six, seven years and then leave after the Pipeline boom. So there's a future here, I figure. There's always going to be growth and construction and more pipelines up here, this is only the first one, so no problem. . . ." There are three proposals for a natural gas pipeline to transport Prudhoe gas to market, for several mineral slurry lines in the Brooks Range, and oil lines from the Naval Petroleum Reserve, and the Kandik Basin.

Pete went over to look at the Automatic Motor Control Teletype unit printout, which had just stopped rapping out information. It was a continuous record of ads by title and time, the time of each song played, and two or three spots in a row before the weather and job listings, the important stuff. The jocks for upcoming programs, the guys with the smooth verbal moves, were scooting around in their new job roles, selecting discs and spots for the programmer to punch into the console's bank of swirling reels, clicking counters, and blinking bulbs.

There are still a few snags though. A precise one-second delay between announcements or tapes must occur for everything to operate seamlessly. As yet, the lag varies from a half second to as much as two seconds, since KIAK's old vintage tape equipment simply doesn't have an accurate device to measure time. So the jocks have been fooling with a grease pencil mark on the tape at different spots; at the moment, exactly seven inches from the end of the last item. They figure that's roughly the amount of tape that goes by in one second.

And the Rough Places Plain

Black dirt stuck to all five fingers. Black loam and clay clung persistently to every wrinkle, oozed obscenely with any movement, crawled and lodged stubbornly under fingernails, agitated in the alcove where the nose meets the eye, eyelids underlined by dark streaks painted there by gloved hands trying to pull the specks away. It looked as though she never slept. Rich damp earth grabbed and was wedded to everything in its primeval collusion with water, a sullen black spell cast upon the whole world. The tundra is a rich Persian carpet arabesque, thousands of knotted grasses and sedges to the inch; a miniature jungle canopy insulating the permafrost just below from the sun. But break the surface growth, and black and terra-cotta mud oozes from the wound with a bleeder's vengeance. In it, everything sinks.

Sheila scraped the mud off her pants and gloves again. A stream of water spouted off her yellow rain slicker's hood and plummeted into a little pool of its own creation in the meter by a meter square of bare roots and browned cobbles still held by the dark loam. She shivered again, tightened the hood, wiggled each foot in turn to circulate sluggish blood. All day in a meter-square garden set off by measured metal stakes and string, numbered, labeled and recorded in the map of the glacial kame or hillock being charted by surveyors. The next square over was disturbed by an arctic ground squirrel that exited from its nest hole to try to make off with a couple of artifact envelopes recently filled and identified by numbers and names, to steal back some tiny stones untouched for thirteen thousand years, to use the labels for lining nests against the impending cold.

Sodden archaeologists looked up from their travail in the bogs to peer east through the mist. No one said anything, yet everyone felt the presence of another creature nearby. Two caribou cantered up, froze, watched. Their spring-loaded antelope gait propelled them clockwise around the mound of gravel left by a Pleistocene glacier, the pious, wary circumambulation of Hindu pilgrims to a Himalayan shrine. Men have watched caribou from that hundred-foot-high hill ever since it was formed, and obtained sustenance from the swollen Porcupine caribou herd of several hundred thousand that passes this spot every year, without fail. Fog seeped in from the northwest, and whisked the caribou away.

The crew foreman bellowed again: "Hey! Location twelve! Hey, wake up!" An outlying group of three sloshed within sight shortly, numbed, eyes all asleep, shell shocked from exposure to the insatiable driving dampness. "Hey, how you folks doing? . . . Jesus, this is really a bitch today, huh. . . . Break time. Everybody's been in the tent for twenty minutes already. Janet, you look really awful, c'mon let's get some coffee. . . ." Earl Cromwell, the foreman, waddled away in his rain gear with the three docilely in tow, not a flicker in any eye. He wore a Greenland anorak, tattered and embroidered, that had traveled all the places he had, and carried his tall, muscular frame about with a slight limp. With the reddish beard that flowered into a blond mustache and the ever-present digging trowel in his left hand, Earl was perfect for a Canadian Club advertisement, drawing heavily on the collective image of an arctic wildlife biologist at work in the field.

On the other side of the kame near the break tent, a couple of reptilian dirt buggies dumped gravel at the end of a narrow causeway of fill stretching south toward the nearest camp but never reaching anything, overtaken by the mists. Roaring, smoking replicas of armor-plated monsters from archaic times plucked straight out of an academy of natural science, their ancient habitat torn from the display case as well. Nothing could be that big, that violently carnivorous, groaning through the mire croaking diesel songs, whining all the while.

Periodic diesel belches announced the arrival of another load of gravel in one of the thirty-four-cubic-yard dumptrucks or thirty-ton Wabco Haulpaks slithering along the Haul Road creeping north from Toolik and south from Happy Valley. Any slight elevation, each pile of rocks and dirt, was strip-mined for fill; there was never enough. Slope Mountain, just to the west of the separate pipe and road routes, was suffering continual abuse. A pack of D-8 cats and loaders worked an incredible switchbacked course up the two-thousand-foot face of the peak, blasting out and tearing into the strata to reach the upper terraces of rubble. The work crew high on the face rapped out its staccato counterpoint

of sharp blasts and soprano diesel arias in every hour of the day. By night, the raving, clacking fantasies continued, lit by floodlights, nurtured by darkness.

A ten-person Bell 205 helicopter buzzed the kame a hundred feet off the ground, hoping for a quick glance at the ladies, as usual. It circled, jammed all other thoughts like the hell-bent presses of the Anchorage *Times,* and called on the field unit to see if the archaeologists needed anything. Alyeska was charged — by virtue of the National Antiquities Act of 1906 — with supplying all necessities and logistics for the teams scattered along the route's entire length, searching for artifacts that would otherwise be destroyed. Pankaj, a sometime student and man of affairs from India who rather artfully interwove drama and anthropology, grabbed the radio and called in the order of the day to the hovering $600-an-hour craft: "Hello! Double-O Whiskey? Ahh, yeah we've got a couple of requests. Can you pick us up six dustpans back in camp? Yeah, you know . . . dustpans like the sweeping-the-floor type? Oh, and how about some fresh donuts, yeah, but only if that new baker in town has plucked a fresh batch out'a the oven this afternoon. We like the cherry Danish best. . . . Shantih . . . shantih . . . shantih."

"Pankaj, what the hell was that last stuff?" Earl bellowed, his own brand of diplomacy. Very competitive, stand there and simply tell people what he was thinking, challenging quietly.

"Oh. Shantih. That's the way we always end our invocations to the Gods. . . . It's, ahh, about four thousand years old. Seems to work pretty well . . ."

Ten minutes later, a different chopper alighted and snatched away one of the women. Ostensibly for an emergency phone call; the pilots were always coming up with some new line or other to augment the ordinary "Okay baby, we're not setting down until you kick in. . . ." Three or four hours later Marie returned in the enormous aviary, cheerful and accompanied by another crate of Maine lobster, despite her meek protests that there were two cases — at $300 a case — in the mess tent already for the eleven "ologists." Marie assured everyone that all was well. It was just an old boyfriend of hers who had called her home on the South Shore of

Boston, nothing special; heard she was in Alaska, tried the number in Fairbanks for the hell of it, got referred, and was amazed to get through to someone eighty miles from the nearest village, two hundred and seventy miles from the nearest road. The call cost "Uncle Al" about $1600 someone figured. In another hour, the first chopper showed up again with a fourth case of lobster, $1200 worth now in camp, as there was plenty in the Toolik commissary. There was an unofficial rule that no two tasks be accomplished on any one trip. The pilots are paid flight-time differential, and underpaid at that. Nothing like a war in the jungles to provide an inexpensive corps of unemployed pilots. Good, too, nothing bothered them, flying in quicksilver fogs at dusk, bucking winds in tight gorgeous ravines, when the winter's cold forced metal fatigue into everybody's consciousness and the bosses debated grounding all craft. The choice was the pilots' officially, up to their judgment, but those who balked never seemed to get back from R&R. Competition within their oppressed class worked to the advantage of Alyeska and Bechtel; pilots traded stories of money and favorable reassignments from the camp honchos as rewards to the pilots who flew when the skies were mean.

Some of them found time for helicopter hunting when things were slow, spotting runs up valleys to sight caribou and brown bear and wolves, then flying in real fast to strafe them or land and shoot a while. It was hard on the animals, and highly illegal. Chasing a barren ground caribou with a chopper for only a mile could consume more calories than the animal could possibly replace, given the poor grazing land in this polar desert, six to eight inches of rain a year. Yet water everywhere because of the permafrost.

The mammals of the Slope kept vigil over the mechanized insanities, the grunting, poking around, digging into everything. Two surveyors were accosted by a rabid fox when out with the transit and rod south of Happy Valley. As it was a pretty good looking red fox, with one of those marvelous tails, they wanted to hang onto the pelt. So, they skinned it, and somehow somebody official back in Toolik heard about it. After all, everybody goes everywhere by chopper, and word gets around through the information-broker pilots. The camp physician's assistant had them immediately flown out to Fairbanks for the notorious set of fourteen injections in the solar plexis. Upon returning to camp weeks later, they were fined $500 by the state for poaching, since no hunting or firearms were allowed within five miles of the right-of-way for the Pipeline or the Haul Road. Another tale of foxes and workers in the years of 1973-1974 when the rabies epidemic on the Slope, nature's mechanism for periodic population control among predators of arctic hare and lemmings, was at its height. Mammals on the Slope are intricately tied to the quixotic death migrations of the brown lemming. When the lemmings leave en masse for their ultimate appointment with the sea, the snowy owls and arctic and red foxes and wolves move out with them, whole caravans of creatures changing course together, flushing the willow gulleys winding north because of instinct and interdependency. The Slope will be barren of their cries and gaits for years, until the lemmings swell in number again and begin to feel their self-corrective urge.

Michael Baker, Jr., Inc. is responsible for the soil engineering work on the road. Everybody in the outfit is from the head office in Jackson, Mississippi, so a little grits-and-home-fries ghetto has sprung up in the arctic. They all wear a uniform of hog-farm oversized overalls and yellowed thermal underwear or Penny's flannel plaid, with blossoming peach orchard grins. Always contently cooking dirt in their little shack, flying around the surveyors' stakes for samples, reading Zap comics and soiled novels. The office is lined with Pan Am's vision of life in Hawaii and Rio, the luxurious hotels rising like bright white bunkers defending the beaches of places they'll never know. Otherwise, only tired, iron-poor Levittown tinges and hues.

The dining hall is life. "Yeah, there's a lot of money to be made here all right, if I can just keep my mind in the right place. . . ." Two Eskimo welder's helpers across the table wandered on in their choppy sea, frozen-jawed tongue full of abrupt cutoffs and sled dog barks. A kid nursing his first beard, who looked like he was cut from dough with a cookie cutter, stood up,

seized his over-loaded tray, and dumped the contents over an antagonist's head.

A red-haired carpenter talked about his last gig, up in "Giggly Gulch." They were building a launderette. The carpenters methodically erected it in the chosen spot, and put in two-by-ten joists topped with three-quarter-inch plywood as support platforms for the washers and dryers. Then the foreman for the local Alaskan subcontractor came along and said no, those are supposed to be on the other side of the building. So they rebuilt the platforms there that afternoon. The next day, the representative from Bechtel, general contractor for the camps north of the Yukon, happened by to inform the carpenters that those were the old plans, and that the washers go on the other side, the initial platform location. They ripped up the studs again, rebuilt the platforms and settled down for a union designated coffee break, their sense of humor paled by the bureaucratic indecisiveness on such a minor point. By then the resident Happy Valley Alyeskans had heard about the problem and sent over the assistant camp manager to settle the dust. He arrived to inform the crew that the entire building was in the wrong spot and that a water tank was supposed to go there by the newest plan. The crew rallied one last time to rebuild the structure twenty feet over to the west before the foreman "dragged up" and caught the five o'clock flight to Fairbanks. He was in the union hall two days later, trying to get back out.

The busiest room in camp was left of the entrance to the dining hall. It served consecutive sentences as library of beagle-eared westerns and sleezy novels and a growing set of educational cassettes; gambling casino, all eyes turned to the nightly proceedings and staggering proceeds; and chapel for a fly-by-night aviator-parson. Three sideshows on a ten-by-twelve stage, for free.

A German named Wolfgang had just arrived from Galbraith. Word got around that he traveled up and down the Line camps playing serious poker, and could just about always cash anybody's paycheck with his winnings from the $25-a-bet no-limit poker games. Wolfgang stayed his usual couple of weeks until he'd cleaned out the camp, and then quit before R&R to relocate.

The battle between the forces of good and evil took on a curious immediacy, as Lindsey Williams, "The Flying Parson . . . On Wings of Witness With the Lord" according to his business card, gave sermons at seven P.M. on Tuesdays and the following mornings at eight. To close one week's sermon to the Bible study group meeting in the tiny room, the window held open by a can of Copenhagen snuff, the leader announced that he would "like to read from Isaih:40, The Book of the Consolation of Israel, about making the rough places plain; well, that's the way the Standard version goes, this one's a little different."

The Calling of the Prophet

A Voice cries, "Prepare in the wilderness
a way for Yahweh.
Make a straight highway for our God
across the desert.
Let every valley be filled in,
every mountain and hill be laid low,
Let every cliff become a plain,
and the ridges a valley;
then the glory of Yahweh shall be
revealed and all mankind shall see it;
for the mouth of Yahweh has spoken."
A voice commands: "Cry!"
and I answered, "What shall I cry?"
– "All flesh is grass
and its beauty like the wild flower's.
The grass withers, the flower fades
when the breath of Yahweh blows on them.
[The grass is without doubt the people.]
The grass withers, the flower fades,
but the word of our God remains for ever."

102

Abandoned water pipe
from Gold Rush

They were blasting on Slope Mountain again. Hundreds of tons of limestone avalanched down the terraced contour toward the State Road, and the cluster of canvas tents alongside the glacial kame. "Terrible Bob" McMillan was dozing in his D-8 cat despite all the noise the out-of-tune engine made, despite the high winds. His cat was suspended down the steep face by a three-hundred-foot steel cable, attached at the top to another D-8. While the trucks and Wabcos were loading, there was nothing to do but dangle and wait; any movement would start new slides onto the vehicles just below. And try to think about anything but the god-awful headache and general nausea, like poison had been pumped into every artery after another four A.M. night, partying with the boys, fourth or fifth in a row.

Rock crashed in a storm of dust to the terrace below where the trucks loaded. Two Bell Rangers dropped from the very summit straight down the face at a hundred and fifty miles an hour, buzzing barely a hundred feet over the cats and the laborers below. An hour later a random cacophony of unrehearsed explosions ripped limestone bedrock from the bottom of a placid ancient sea. It was a war on the form of the land, a struggle to make it conform to some engineer's vague notion of how it should be.

The Haul Road was a concession made by Alyeska to the state's expansionist tendencies under former Governor Egan, and was not authorized by the Pipeline Act of 1973. The first bridging of the Yukon River into an integral wilderness undivided in any way had begun for the Pipeline. And, possibly, to open the Brooks to copper ore trucks and the five bus companies that had already applied for "Certificates of Public Convenience and Necessity" to haul the overflow from Disneyland and Florida to the Arctic Ocean. The string of abandoned Pipe camps would become outposts on what would be billed as another great adventure like the Trans-Siberian Railroad, or the road west through the Cumberland Gap. Yet the Haul Road may remain closed to the public indefinitely, on the governor's recommendation. It represents one of the finest statements of the classic Alaskan paradox of development: any action that encourages growth and improvement of the living standard also concomitantly tends to destroy the unique and cherished life-style in the state by utilizing the very resources and potential that are the foundation of its uniqueness. Development is a package deal in which one cannot easily separate the benefits from the deep costs associated with them.

In a road-building machine, a man becomes immortal. He can tear into hillsides, torture the beast to no end without retort, do things he has feverishly dreamed of. "Terrible Bob," ex-World Champion Rodeo Cowboy and with a belt buckle to prove it, pushed stone around all day, rolled it down the face. It wore out the steel teeth welded onto the blade to prevent grinding on the blade itself, which suffered sadistic abuse without a murmur. Horrible screeching steel on rock, bellowing black diesel snarls, huge hydraulic arms of iron moving barriers all day till the shift ends or they drop and are discarded. At the end of the day, McMillan would often scold the others for their indifference, and felt that the way a man handles his rig mimics the way he is to his buddies. Then he'd put on his air force snorkle parka with the Fairbanks "Tundra Trompers" off-the-road vehicle club patch sewn on the right shoulder and crash down the rutted road to camp.

On the fourth of August, their work forcefully curtailed, Earl Cromwell and the last four archaeologists tore down their gridwork of stakes and strings and the checkerboard of burial plots on the bluff at Oksrukoyik, where two rivers meet. A settlement of hunters had been established briefly, then just as it must have been, the pits and refuse beside them were abandoned to move on to better game. The scrapers and D-9s reached the spot the next morning and strip-mined the entire several-hundred-yard-long bluff. The road had reached south from Happy Valley.

Nigel Worthington was on loan to Alyeska from a parent company and ruled his road section headed south like a field marshal. The helicopter had barely set down when he hopped out of the door brandishing blueprints and his best strictly business smirk. Fresh from consultations, he demanded a faster pace from the survey archaeologists who tested each gravel borrow site and then gave formal clearance. Pink Oxford shirt with collar buttoned, thin-waisted belt, stylish safari boots, he was the epitome of the well-dressed Victorian explorer in the wilds. "Just get us some fill okayed, and we'll show that Toolik bunch how to build a road! You ologists never seem to understand — we're here to build a road."

Earl Cromwell nodded, his usual response to that comment. "Say, what'd you people decide to do about the peregrine falcons the biologist found up by Franklin?" State and federal wildlife monitors had demanded that the road be relocated for some eighteen miles at an estimated cost of about three million dollars. Nigel and his sidekick from Bechtel, an overweight crewcut ex-marine in khakis tucked into Vietnam jungle boots and a black baseball hat, both agreed that the move was absurd. Earl ignored the comments, and struck up with Nat, the Head Eskimo In Charge as everybody called him, a token Native in middle management as logistics engineer for Morrison-Knudson. They walked around the site watching the crew of archaeologists moving on hands and knees like a squad of varicose-veined scrub ladies, whisk brooms in hand. Nat asked quietly, "If a peregrine is worth three quarters of a million, how much is a barber in Valdez worth? This is killing *his* life-style, too. Ecological damages are a safe, tangible disaster that we can easily deal with, easily quantify, so private industry can be forced into doling out funds for reforestation, for falcons, and rabbits. But what when a whole community, an entire ecosystem of *people*, is disrupted, or an entire race is being exterminated? That's harder for everyone to deal with. Too hot; no one wants to touch it. That's what's happening to the Eskimo people, to my people in Wales, my family. We need *social* impact statements written, too, goddammit; the ecology stuff is a good first step, but we've got to see towns and people in the same way, as interconnected systems that we can't toy with. . . . Hey, got to go, Nigel's getting restless. Drop by after dinner in camp if you can catch a chopper on in . . ."

Earl and short stocky Nat kept on talking later in the dining hall. Nat had taken his engineering degree in Seattle and was hired by M-K in a capacity he felt unqualified for but willing to try. "Well, it might as well be me as anybody, they just want a Native in there to point to when the feds come around. But I think that most of the policies of the government as far as education is concerned have to do with destroying the families, and I don't understand it. The schools aren't doing the job, goddammit! You get a kid for twelve years and that son of a bitch isn't educated. Now why not? Now you take an Eskimo and you can get him in a village and the goddamn Eskimo will learn from his grandmother and grandfather, and by the time that kid is six years old he'll have damn near perfected his language, I mean *perfected* it!

"I think we could take this goddamned pressure off and create a beautiful world. I think we could create a good life. I don't give a shit if someone paid me an electrician's wages at twenty-two dollars an hour, and I earned what I figured out today is about a hundred and twenty thousand dollars a year. Really! I'm not living a good life here. Do you see any families? One thing I really miss, you know, like children, and families. And babies! And cats and dogs and animals. You know, all these things that create a balance of life. Suddenly all these things are gone and here we are in these sterile rooms. And this is only a reflection of all the things going on beyond this camp. It's becoming very, very sterile. I think we need to get involved with an entirely new plan, a whole new concept. This goddamn world needs to depressure itself before everyone starts blowing each other up. That's another nice thing about Eskimos too, that they don't believe in competition. If you want to move off, you want to do something, do it! No one's going to get in your way. No one's going to criticize you either." Nat had been drinking a lot of coffee, but had wanted to talk anyway.

"I don't know, I'm really upset with the world. Any time you take a place like Alaska and take billions of dollars and get all these goddamn machines in here and destroy the earth, and say that you're doing it to create a better life, it's bullshit! You don't destroy something to make something better. Look at the energy picture here in camp. These goddamn trucks out here, look at the inefficiency, at the goddamn fuel they burn! I know of a good many people just in this goddamned camp, girls that are secretaries or god knows what, all of their goddamned money is supporting their goddamned car! Some of those people are living a half a dozen different lives! You can't do that and keep it together. I don't understand these people, I really don't. What is success? Jesus Christ, why don't we just throw that word success away and just strive for happiness, something that's simple. Something we understand, something we're in control of. People are suffering from Future Shock. They don't know what the game is going to be next year. Now, look at the Eskimo society. Say I'm twenty years older, have, say, ten or twelve kids. I've got it made! 'Cause all my kids are out hunting and fishing and take care of me. That's your retirement plan and your happiness. Old people are considered a burden to white man's capitalism. It's becoming a very harsh world.

"You ought to see my nice skin, my hair, my eyes, my entire body. Then I come out here and eat that goddamned food. I'm a product of that goddamned forced-fed beef! It's the quality of life, more and more money, it's continuing to erode. You talk about, you know, a one billion dollars for our last space shot to Mars. Yet we had to fight like a fuckin' tooth and nail up here for our one billion dollars for our claims settlement. If your problems are bad, our problems are ten times worse.

"Eskimos can't handle the English language. They *speak* it well, but you get them involved in reading and writing, and numbers, and physics, and applying that knowledge to a job to make money, and they simply can't adjust to it. You can't do it in just twenty years; it doesn't work. The unions have training programs, but they aren't recruiting. You've got to go to the village and hand carry that son of a bitch; you've got to take care of him. They learn very slowly in English, but could learn how to operate heavy equipment instantly in Eskimo. But even then they still don't understand the construction operation and how to coordinate activities, they're not going to be able to hack it. In our family of ten kids, we've got one kid who's got the brains to hack it in the white man's world, and do it successfully. I'll encourage him to do it, but the others couldn't hack it.

"Eskimos are more involved in needing money now, because of fuels to heat with and hunt; the average utility bill is about two hundred dollars a month. They've given up, they're apathetic. My family has given up. Jesus Christ, I just got a letter from my wife today. We've all kinds of problems up there, you know. Listen, like this: 'How's my ding a ling ling doing over on the other side of the world. Sure seems like you'd been gone forever. Sure miss you a lot.' These letters come every week. 'Received the hundred dollars today and the picture of you. Baby just woke up I don't think he'll let me sleep tonite. I wrote you about five page letter but I tore them all up. I burned three full pages of really weird letter I wrote. Baby haven't been feeling well for so long he's got cold for months now. He even had to have shots for three days. That really pisses me off I wonder why I always say I don't want to move over there to the big town over there.' That's what she calls Fairbanks, how she refers to it, the big town. 'I always want to move out of this place. I'm the only one supporting the whole family. Dad's cousin from White Mountain hang himself. But they took the dead body here to Wales. Because he was raised in Wales. He first stole two thousand dollars from one of the stores in White Mountain. He didn't even spend one cents from the money. The troopers from Nome went to White Mountain even though they found him guilty they let him go. The next day his father found him hanging next to there house. And one guy Annie Clicker's brother the one working at Bering Straits' — that's our regional corporation — 'her brother try to shoot himself. And he did but he's alive. Now for the bad sad part of my whole letter. I regret why you even send it so fast its because you love me I know. Mom ask me if I could give them $99.00 for food stamps. Anyway I gave it to her and then soon as I said I should go down to Peabody's and buy a Maytag Washer she started saying we sure need motor gas to hunt so I was mad went over to the store I had credit I owed 60.00 I had to buy them food. I gave them 40.00 to buy gas. Now then I didn't even eat all day so I went to the store now I have only $2.50 dollars in my pocket. I hope you don't kill me but I'm very depressed myself. I hope you forgive me. My cousin

Fairbanks

Debby Wright gave me this twenty. She said for you to send her twenty dollars worth of Marjiana. I wouldn't mind smoking some myself. Richie Harris still does the rock n roll sometimes. He really play really cool far out music. You should always be careful when you're working. I know you're homesick Hon. Just make me sick you being so far from home. Really missing you're warm body keeping me warm. I think I'll die when I see you. It's seems like you've gone to Siberia or Russia. I was really tempted to go to Fairbanks last week. Thought you'd never go back to work so I didn't. Mom and them caught a big bull moose when they went hunting they had four shares. Our freezer is full of moose, blue berries, salmon berries. Sure enjoying eating meat. Fish almost all summer sure got tired of it. Please come home soon Nat. I don't need that money so much as I need you. . . .' You know? Things are really falling apart out there. This is an average family. If anybody has any goddamned money, everybody's trying to rip them off. They don't want a bottle of whiskey, they want a case." Nat put the letter away, he had nothing else to say.

Alaska is ripe with visionaries, the ones with clear, dark vision that see the real nature of things, and know the course events will take. Most of them restrict their visions to bite-sized chunks of real estate or reality — their homestead's hundred and sixty acres, gonna be a motel and package store some day, by gawd; a personal gold claim that'll pay in a few years, mark my word. Alaska is a state of mind, not of the Union, a catalog of slightly swollen desires, a compendium of souls in pursuit of them. But most of the ones with the visions just calmly carry on their way, the hard drivers forging miniature cities from their trailer homes; the mad, the sage old trappers who talk to the Northern Lights, in such a way that they answer back.

Some, though, are empire builders and devise vast plans that affect everyone, like erecting skyscrapers and filling in bays. When it's only a few lots here and there then let them meddle, but designing the lives of others is not a chore for self-made men, those saints and witches both, to be revered for their diligence but burned for their quest for power. The scale of the operation says it all in Alaska and always has. As soon as the gold strikes became mechanized and supported by Outside capital, it was instantly a different game, another big company running the show. The modest entrepreneur is sacred, but the massive-scale operations and the men with big dreams are anathema. May it always be that way, may the splendid Alaskan anarchy continue in cooperation with the state and federal planners.

Toolik is a small western town transported to another planet, replete with the strip-mine indifference to visual chaos and mechanical breakdowns. Earlier generations of tractors are still lying where they died, a straightforwardness lost in middle-class suburbia, where things rust or swim behind fences. An elderly black man — facial furrows and cheek bones charcoaled in with the ash of all the camp — works all day at the incinerator on the edge of town, glowing yellow inferno matching the tint of his M-K hard hat. The armored incinerator sits serenely on horizonless tundra, a towering furnace burning incessantly in a wasteland that offers nothing it can consume. It burns day and night.

Plenty of news from the outside world comes into this floating space station by regular flights, but none of it is immediate or really believable: riots in Bangkok, riddles in Washington. Someone says all the papers are printed bogusly and shipped in. Both dinner and breakfast are served up to seven A.M. and seven P.M. for the workers beginning or ending the twelve-hour shifts. Mist and space conspire to suspend the passage of time; three hundred and twenty people float on in a field of sense deprivation, awaiting rumors of shuttle flights to other points named but unknown.

There is no actual frontier or borderline that marks the Pipeline's farthest penetration into the tundra, only a series of little intrusions into the silence. The tundra North Slope is Alaska's Great Plains, its Sahara and Siberia. Space . . . there are no parts or boundaries, just the whole. Stratofortress weather fronts move in a sweeping full-dress display across the pastel solitude, contained only by the snow and limestone Brooks Range, splayed to the south like the blanched backbones of once-loping caribou found scattered in the tussocks. The foothills just twenty miles north have their own charcoal solemnity to them, a banker's suit broken only by the thin stripes of snow gulleys reaching down to the valleys: first broad with the reminder of winter, then faint silver streams of meltwater continuing below.

And the Great Weather, the traveling might floating high above, brings its own definite dark hues in shadows cast forever, whole herds migrating across the ginger and mustard tone that the eye assigns to the tundra when viewed from afar. Nearby summits at sunset glow in tawny, then ochre, then pasta-like hues, until finally the phantom peaks merge with the slate sky that arises far beyond. When we catch a glimpse of a whole that is greater than its parts, a unity flushed out all at once, we are apt to blush sacred crimson, or attain the ashen reverence reserved for clear manifestations of deity, yet it is always here.

Alaska itself is a P. T. Barnum circus and traveling show, a curio display of giant and minuscule travesties of the real world. Somehow the oddities of a continent have all migrated to its far corner, dwarf duchesses, elephants, and audiences of children. There are the tiny tundra miniatures of things that grow man-sized elsewhere: dwarf dogwoods, rhododendrons and roses, fragile, bizarre and blessèd. The tundra, while at first seeming featureless, has enormous expression in its tussocks and depressions, all the cluttered chaos: tiny fox droppings, a broken petal of sphagnum moss, three buds as yet unfurled. Hugeness cries out, as well, in freak hulking glaciers, mammoth mountains and world-record-class big game.

In other lands, the size of man is the basic unit of measure, and objects with roughly his proportions —

trees, houses, boulders — occupy the middle distance. On the Slope, a worker is alone in a sea of extremes of scale. A crush and questioning of identity occurs, too big a task for many people to design and build a world between the arctic poppies and the twenty-thousand-foot heights of Denali. The land is carnivorous, for space allows things to be seen all alone, it compels naked honesty and essence; it searches out what they are.

People feel inferior to the immensity and indifference of the natural world here, humble and trying hard, but failure is fully tolerated in old-time Alaska. Feel the way slowly; one need not produce results here, no one will mind, so go gently now. Quality, not speed, is the password. Alaska has been a land of experience, allowing work toward the solution of problems without the expectation of success. It's as if the people sought a physically intimidating world of overwhelming proportions, too big to tackle or fear failure in, a world that graphically and physically represents all the complexities found at home Outside, in urbane dilemmas. Almost as if the people needed to have some everpresent reminder that the problem is big and will take a very long time to surmount. Maybe forever. No worry now, there is always tomorrow.

Alaska touches those who visit through her gates; she leaves her mark. It is not a note of recognition, or a sign of graduation, for there are no milestones along her trails. That, itself, is the mark left — the lack of measurements, the absence of signs to see how far one has come. There are few subdivisions of the whole, and one must look hard to see where the valley slips off to become the hill. After a few years, one simply ceases searching; it's all the same right outside the cabin door. When one has stopped the phantom quest for other places, since Alaska is the end of the road, and lived well in just one, then it is time to claim residence.

It is the space, the utter totalitarian vastness, that has allowed this slow, exploratory life-style to exist. So the task of the visitor on the Slope is to explore the huge range of openness, to learn how to relate the bit of lichen flake to the dark, vast storm front staggering in from the south.

The glacial kame beneath Slope Mountain was an obvious choice for a survey archaeologist in search of sites. It had been discovered several years earlier by a graduate student covering the proposed route for Alyeska, when — after numerous cups of coffee — he found it necessary to be set down immediately from the helicopter. Before the chopper had finished landing, the two archaeologists realized that this was a rich site: there were unusually large blades and fragments scattered all over the surface. Nothing like them had been recovered anywhere else in the state, and a new type was hesitantly introduced to the scholarly world, based in part on preliminary radiocarbon dates of about 10,000 to 12,000 B.P. (before the present). Luck rather than logic had played a great role in the location of the Pipeline route.

"I don't care what anybody says, I still like the looks of a nice arrowhead," Earl remarked, fondling a freshly unearthed point of baleen-black obsidian, uncommon in the area. Everyone crowded around to admire. "Never outgrew it, eh Earl?" Pankaj chided. "No, guess I never did," Earl admitted with a shy smile, eyes twinkling and his flaming beard cocked a bit to the side.

Archaeologists live the schizophrenic life of most Alaskans, roaming and digging in out-of-the-way places all summer, and then retreating into the labs and libraries to analyze the finds and develop theoretical models through the long winters. Days in the field worked the same way, troweling in the daylight, and then writing up notes and bagging artifacts in the evening. There were lots of late-night puns about the infamous "Arctic Small Tool Tradition" over Hudson's Bay 151 proof Demerara rum — "distilled in Guyana, bottled in Britain" — smuggled in under the aegis of "Archaeological Supplies." Sea chanties and Scottish ballads capped the evening. Practically everyone in the crew with a serious interest in archaeology was fascinated with the idea of handicraft and living off the land. They talked about crude fiber blankets, baskets, portable hide boats, and the different schools of thought on sharpening one's trowel. Flintnapping, the art of devising usable tools from chunks of rock, entered conversation regularly, as it "is kind of fun to do, and a good way to release frustrations out back of the house when the analysis isn't going too well. Like that guy in France who keeps a hundred pounds of flint in his backyard to explode into." Basically, they were curious but not necessarily practicing artisans trying to uncover the history of man's relationship to his environment, to realign man and his natural world. Archaeologists are environmentalists of a sort, though not in the political arena, with the same nostalgia for the vision of an integrated, organic way of life on the land, the way it always must have been.

"Jesus! I can't figure out how some band of hunters could've lived here off and on for thirteen thousand years," Earl yelled to a colleague, above the roar of a giant scraper dumping dirt for the Haul Road two hundred feet away, "and it takes us three summers to find out where the hell they were on one tiny hill. Ten thousand years from now they'll sure know where Toolik and the Pipe were." Earl and Raymond, another archaeologist prominent in the contract work for Alyeska let out to the University of Alaska, joined in a long shouting dialogue that eventually degenerated into diatribe. They talked about the beautiful, tiny tools they'd been collecting for several summers, the incredible craftsmanship involved in each one, the way they fitted the hand perfectly and gave it teeth to cut with, all the lagoons and miniature cirques and valleys found in the conchoidal fractures in the mudstone and obsidian. The two big men were working together in adjacent squares to uncover a dense mass of waste flakes, ancient days' sharpening of blades dulled on fresh caribou meat. He must have sat in precisely the same spot and posture, using a piece of bone or another stone to flake a cobble of mudstone into an artisan's knife for notching ivory. Every point was artfully made, the form lying hidden within the chosen stone first intuited and then released by the hunter's hands: what lies within, he'd ask . . . ah, yes, scraper! The two men paused for a moment to look up at the Brooks Range twenty miles south, a serrated mouth of incisors set on edge in a vast plain that swallows everything. In the break tent, the coffee was ready. Someone broke open a fresh carton of five hundred red and white striped plastic stirring rods, and passed the packets of sugar around.

"Yeah, the trick in survey archaeology is to pretend you're a Nunamiut, become one, and wander around the way he would've, then you'll naturally end up in the right spots," Earl began. "But it was real different here, we've overlooked lots of good sites. This is a whole different ballgame than academic research. The selection of sites . . ." "Hah! Selection?" Raymond replied, "Yah, right — the sites are wherever they're building. It's all in a professional capacity now, it's a business proposition. . . ." Raymond was quiet and reclusive, but like Earl ready to accept any challenge, academic or otherwise. "This is of course a major test site for developing new techniques to deal with this type of public archaeology. It's business, not the stodgy twenty years of analysis before publishing the results of excavation. There's incredible pressure on us now to produce, to rip the stuff out of the ground and turn in a report, financed by Alyeska, in a measly nine months after closing down for the winter. Salvage archaeology they call it, rip and run, make good money, do the best job possible in a couple of months and then turn it over to the graders for road fill. Too bad if you've got any additional questions when you get back to the lab. Well, this site's about rounded up. Pretty unbelievable at first, wasn't it? All those huge, incredibly crude blades lying all over. But after developing that first hypothesis and learning enough to scrap it, it looks like you've got it all tied together now. From a preliminary, primitive study of the patterns of distribution, to a good working horizontal stratigraphy that sets up some kind of sequence of occupancy . . ."

Earl smiled. "Yeah, as long as no one turns up anything conflicting, that kinda worries me at this stage in the game, when we've got it pretty much worked out — Hey, you people doing Location Six, don't find any-thing over there, okay?" he half-joked. "That would really blow it . . ."

Once outside of the forty-man army tent, they realized a Supercub on floats was buzzing the tent and about to set down in the modest lake a couple of hundred feet away. It landed upwind, braking hard to avoid the far shore, and quickly reversed direction to drift back toward the tent in the persistent breeze. Two men simply jumped off the floats into the thigh-deep chilled water before it ceased sailing, and waded ashore.

"Howdy! Where you guys from?" somebody queried. "Naknek." "Ah, where's that?" "Naknek. Near Dillingham. Just flew up here." From Bristol Bay, fifteen hundred miles to the southwest.

They stayed a half hour for coffee and warmth, to talk of the poor salmon runs that had led to Nixon's official declaration of Bristol Bay as a disaster area, the poaching Korean and Japanese trawlers still plying the waters, the hunting guide and fisherman-senator from Naknek who was running for governor in the November election. Jay Hammond — "one of us, tough, damned good fisherman. Cares about the little folks like you and me not the big oil companies and real estate bandits that Egan's one of. . . . He really knows his shit, too. . . . Been a drinking buddy of mine for years" — Hammond had just won the Republican nomination over former governor and big businessman Wally Hickel. A conservationist legislator who read his own poems into the Senate record, full bearded and eyes like tempered steel: full of life and determination. Sheep hunting season began in four days, so they were spotting herds in precipitous gorges before the clients arrived. As mysteriously as they came, they went off into the night to Bettles, staging area for Brooks Range expeditions.

David and Tam Ketscher run the Bettles Trading Post just on the edge of the airstrip. They came up to Alaska in 1972 from Fresno, California, not far from Yosemite Valley, where Dave spent a great deal of his free time roaming the vertical desert of several-thousand-foot granite walls with other rock climbers. During 1969 and 1970 a whole new wave of immigration into Alaska occurred, people escaping the urban and student riots, the war in Vietnam, and everything the country was coming to.

Dave left California to live in the Alaskan Bush. He has a twenty-mile-long trapline, and runs it every winter with his dog team and sled, collecting pelts of martin, fox, wolf, wolverine. The pelts hang in his store for sale, or are made into parkas and ruffs and whatnot for the family. The store is doing well despite their newness to the business and a few early mistakes. They were living in a trailer while Dave worked on a cabin, floating logs downstream from a site dozens of miles away where there were large trees, a task that won him considerable respect in town. Bettles straddles two worlds. It is right near the timberline, the northernmost reach of the boreal forests before they give way to the sweep of the tundra, and the Brooks Range just beyond.

The Brooks Range is the psyche of Alaska, the slightly soiled but compassionate soul of a people and a land suddenly forced to engage the rest of the world. It has been elevated from commonplace cartography into a naked geography of hope, a final, inimitable wilderness incarnate. It is a range of both memory and projection, as the people look at how they have lived here now and in ages past, and what the years ahead will bring.

It was hunting season, and Bettles in fall is virtually a slaughterhouse factory outlet. Hanks of caribou hang from tenpenny nails driven through the sinew, on the sides of sheds holding air freight — Canadian snowmobiles, food, fuel, building supplies — for Anaktuvuk Pass and other villages in the Brooks. Malamutes gobble fresh caribou, blood paints a fresh scarlet coat on everything it touches, high velocity rifles with scopes lean against antlers sawed off the carcass, still covered with muscle and flesh and flies. A hearty mixture of hunters from all over the country wandered around the few buildings in town, busy privately developing their own fantasies of the place, and why they were there. They were waiting for the arrival of their certified professional guide, who offered his services and those of his young apprentices for eight days for the sum of fourteen hundred dollars a head. No guarantee on the weather or luck; bring your own food. A slick hunter from Long Island strolled around with his wife in houndstooth checked pants and freshly shined shoes, amazed there were no trees, talking incessantly about his linoleum business and the upcoming World Series. "You know that foreign guy, is he from another country?" one of the apprentices asked another hunter from Soldotna, on the Kenai peninsula southwest of Anchorage. He and his wife had just come out from three weeks at Wild Lake; they had only planned on two, but their pilot forgot about them until someone missed them at home and called Bettles to inquire. The talk returned to cartridge size, world-record game, wolf psychology, and books on Green River mountain men.

Old Bettles was a mining port, the farthest upstream sternwheelers on the Koyukuk could go with gold mining equipment. In the early fifties, when the landing strip was put in by the Civil Aviation Administration to improve upon a military strip of Second World War vintage, the people left the old town intact, with "antique dealer's delights, tho' they'd get shot if they went in there," to cluster around the new strip and junked military equipment or move to distant villages. It was a classic Alaskan scene, the piles of rusting ruins left by the last boomers; get it and get out fast. The Russians were the first. They decimated the Aleut population with disease and colonial expeditions against the Tlingits, their major competitors in trading. The seal, walrus, and sea otter populations declined immediately upon their arrival. Then the Americans came, and eventually the Gold Rush, when men stripped the soil and washed it in sluiceboxes for the glowing metal, then piled it back up again. The mounds still grow hardly anything; the dredges and towns sit in place, visual scars. Then the military in the war, and finally the oil companies crisscrossing the Slope in cat trains, leaving ruts that grow deeper every year, and thousands of barrels floating on the tundra. The gold that once chained watch to wearer and built city halls is now a black magic, a crude black liquid. Alaska has always been an exploited colony of nonresident business interests and a home for wild men. Whenever useful, the original Native population has been exploited to serve these interests. Otherwise, they've been ignored.

All of the land for miles is legally frozen for the local Evansville Native community, pending land claims settlement. Dave Ketscher had to build his cabin and store on leased state airport land, the only spot close to the passengers. Bettles is a jumping-off point for the whole Brooks Range, and sees a remarkable variety of prospectors grubstaking it all summer on gold claims, government inspectors and investigators of all descriptions, tourists from Miami who collect a certificate — signed by the captain — announcing that they've flown across the Arctic Circle, mountain-mad hunters and climbers and walkers, and all the local Native villagers on their way to and from everywhere else.

Anaktuvuk Pass is located right on the crest of the Divide between two distinct worlds: the jumbled, lightly timbered, wild Brooks Range valleys, and the barren two-hundred-by-a-thousand-mile North Slope, the polar desert. The inland Eskimos there, called Nunamiut, draw on both exotic ecosystems for their staple of caribou and furs. A major portion of the arctic herd of 242,000 caribou moves north to the Slope through Anaktuvuk every spring, and back south to better grazing every fall. The Ketschers trade groceries from the store for caribou-skin masks of Eskimo faces, decorated with various furs, hair, beards, and eyebrows.

"Yes, it helps them out, and we sell them to people like you," Tam replied to a self-proclaimed "landed gentleman" from Maine. The bearded gentleman mentioned that he'd talked to the owner at Lindy's grocery in Fairbanks, who, he reported, said that "'I've been doing this for twenty years now . . . but I think it's a thing of the past . . . they'll be all gone in ten years. . . . Well, old Lindy told me, he said, 'They're not hungry anymore up at Anaktuvuk, with all those food stamps

and other government programs. I paid cash for these masks since they don't need the groceries anymore. . . . Don't know when I'll get any more in — they make them whenever the spirit moves 'em.' It was kind of sad, he'd been at it so long, they're changing their ways and all. Overhunting by a new predator, the oil industry. Maybe I'll buy a couple from you . . . that woman with the red fox ruff, that's it. Yes, they're just made for the tourists now, I guess." He went on to say that Alaska hasn't been so much an economic frontier as a social one, where one can work out any kind of life-style desired, utopian experiments in a land inundated with mystery. He quoted the Bertrand Russell masthead on one of the papers in Fairbanks: "We are not here to make a living, we are here to make a life."

"Look, I've got to get back to the trailer and have got to lock up the store. Are you interested in those masks at all?" Tam interjected. "Thought you were from Maine, anyway . . ."

"Well, yes on both counts. But I've gotten fond of my beard, and am gonna go home and think it over, maybe move on up here and try to get on the Pipeline just to see it, then settle in somewhere. Fine country, superb . . ." The gentleman returned to the only lodge in town, and quickly sprawled out on his baggage to await his flight. The fiftyish aproned cook halted the card game for a moment with several plastic drug vials of gold nuggets and dust from their mine up the river a ways. The gentleman looked at them, asked the price, and waited until everyone's attention was fixed his way. "Oh, jumping junipers! So *that's* what a gold nugget looks like. I saw dozens of those things out at the packer's camp and wondered what they was! . . ." After the uproar, he retired to his huge L. L. Bean army duck Maine Guide zipper duffel bag. Three Anaktuvuk masks were huddled together on the dirty floor of the lodge by his boots and guns and other gear to go home. The masks had no backing; there were eyelids but no eyes, and only a hole for a mouth. A piece of the job listings section of an old newspaper and a broken leather boot-lace showed through.

I'LL GIVE UP MY GUN
WHEN THEY PRY MY COLD DEAD
FINGERS OFF THE BARREL!

ALAN MERRELL
YUKON

Several caribou moved in from the north around the kame by the Haul Road, gracefully hopping through the wet tundra. It was late September, the ground was freezing and light snow had fallen twice already. "Jesus, Ray, what'd you think about the caribou? The road's due to be finished any day now, and they'll be trying to run south right along and across it. Alyeska sort of bought that other study that said they'd make it okay after they didn't like the results of the first one, you probably know those guys who did it . . ."

Raymond grinned and chopped with his trowel six times in rapid succession. Alaskans still practice a form of totemism, identifying with one animal or another, that seems eccentric, at first, until one sees the magic in the bond. "Don't know, no . . . well, they've been doing it since before these old folks were sitting here, a long time. But I don't know, it's too big for me. . . . Not sure anybody'll know till a couple years from now, or ten. Yeah, it's just potting we're doing here and everywhere else," potting — looting by amateurs for the artifacts of commercial value, the anathema of archaeologists. Survey archaeologists were madly flying around all summer, okaying sites because of the Antiquities Act before the ways of the Old People fell before the plans arising all over the state. Roads and dams and an entire new state capital were under way, mining equipment flown into the Brooks by Hercs, plans to mine nickel from Glacier Bay National Monument.

Earl looked like a bawdy warrior in a heroic Icelandic saga in his Greenland parka, brandishing a trowel. His swearing at reports obscured a core mellowness that surfaced whenever the duties slack off and it's just the boys back in Indiana digging in the corn fields on his uncle's farm. "Well, our being around and visible all the time is a constant reminder to those guys of how much this is costing them, and that they've got to take the feds' environmental regulations seriously. It'll be years before they really understand what the hell we're talking about, ecosystems and energy flow and thermals and stream siltation. Man, when they get through with this place, there's not going to be a bump left in the state. It's going to look just like Kansas."

A couple more caribou showed up. Caribou and wolves are the soul of the north country, the essence of wildness, for the freedom and vast space they demand. The rhythms of their lives are set by the seasons, nothing less; they migrate instinctually, without reflection, and tolerate no barriers. Caribou are our only roving bison herds, our link with the gray, uncertain ages when mammals other than man were lord.

They headed south across the Slope to the Brooks Range, that vast spate of emptiness and the sorrow that ensues. There's a crush of liberation in that vastness, and a hoard of denial. Before now, there were no lines anywhere, yet patience and waiting were always necessary; complete interdependence, waiting for the daily flight of the Beaver, full of fuel and food and news from afar. The tundra lacks moderation or compromise. The Slope sits waiting, as if for some glimmer of the inscrutable purpose for which it is so precisely poised: why the flow of space, many wondered, if not to rush some idea or deed to completion?

Fall was coming in. The grasses all glow golden, riot into flaming scarlets, rot to willow-bark brown. As the caribou lope along the tangled skein-net braided river banks.

Darkest,
Lightest Prudhoe

Prudhoe Bay is the point of origin for the Pipeline, and the end of the known world. The transformation of Alaska by oil began in Prudhoe in '68, all of it, and will keep going long after the last drop of oil is drawn from the deep-storage Sadlerochit formation. An entire civilization runs and depends on that oil; oil has made it all that it is. There is a vast liquid archive of life all along the intersection of Slope and sea in the North, all that fantastic array of creeping, soaring biota compressed into a dark, fluid essence, from which an equally dazzling assortment of compounds and desires can be distilled by alchemies anew. A certain appeal exists in the way one dank substance can become so many things; in the energy stored within. Oil produces everything in America.

You've got to be in the wild spurt of a new well, wildcatting out in the fossilized stillness of a desert at midday, to smell the wonder in oil. To hunt and drill God knows how long and see the salt water flowing out, getting darker and slick, feel the gentle murmurs from far within, ripples, then, later, mounting paroxysms, sudden seizure; sense the rhythms of a swelling, soothing force inside so far it can't be seen. The hell with all the scanners and isotopes down the pipe to see what's going on, you've got to see the oil flow up in undulations and flush out all over the parched souls of the men who toil for the blackness stinging their buoyant, bloodshot eyes and soaking Levi's skin tight, gasping on a saline gulp or two, teeth now jet, Alleluia! It's down there . . .

Prudhoe is the land of lost dimensions. It is a vast sea of flatness and sameness, one enormous whole ecosystem left intact. Totality, cohesion, an endless siege of solitude. In summer, Prudhoe is a lush marsh of seabirds' moist cries of delight, lighter than air above the pack-ice floes nudging the shore. Where the land at last allows itself to be sea, a change of state begun in the Brooks Range foothills a hundred and a half miles to the south, gradually grading into the smoothed pebble beaches of Prudhoe.

Charlie Gainsborough, the camp expediter, drives the bus back and forth from Parsons's camps to the airport all day. He served in Aden and Yemen as a British mercenary back in the late '60's and then came to New England shortly thereafter, and lost most of his accent. Now, in another desert, he's still cool and competent in all circumstances, but inclined to escalate situations by his very presence. He likes class-four white water kayaking in competition-class fiberglass boats, "second only to guerrilla fighting for excitement, and a little safer I'd say, too. Don't growl at me, you freaking gearbox, the cold's your problem baby, all yours. . . . Yah, well, playing with radios and airdrops and semi-automatic elephant guns is a lot of fun, provided it's the other guys who get all the casualties. Yemen was great for about fourteen months, fantastic place, wild desert country, sandstone monoliths all over the place, caravans and bloody raving mad sunburned Marxists on camels being strafed by RAF jets, really, it was a terrific game. At least until my buddy bumbled with the rocket launcher one day and got blown all over the canyon. I'll never forget the spot — spraypaint crimson all over the boulders, the whole bloody bunch of steep yellow walls smeared, and a boom that about blew my eardrums out. Christ it wasn't ten feet away. But kayaking, that's really a fast-paced game, and just yourself . . ."

Charlie, trim-bearded and obviously English, a Clydesdale stockiness, drove on into the white-out conditions. Drifting snow blows again. Snow drifts onto the roadways running north-south, so trucks constantly thrust through the broad piles on their way to and from the camps and the actual work sites. Often, they run off the road into the crusty, packed-snow tundra. A truck freezes up and won't start within a few hours at Prudhoe, where the average temperature in winter is around minus thirty-five, without the windchill factor figured in. The wind blows constantly, so that the perceived temperature falls to minus forty-five, to minus seventy-five regularly, and well below minus a hundred much too often, when bare flesh freezes in five or ten seconds.

Alaska's first oil was produced from the Katalla Field located southeast of Cordova in 1902, and the Cook Inlet Basin south and west of Anchorage has produced the majority of the 700 million barrels of total state oil production, and the 743 billion cubic feet of gas production. Peak production was reached in the state's oil fields in 1970 and is expected to continue at a slow decline until the Prudhoe Bay Field oil production begins in mid-1977, or so the oil industry maintains. When the 1.2-million-barrels-a-day initial capacity of the Pipeline begins to flow to the Terminal in Valdez, oil production in the state will increase five-fold.

Development drilling in the Prudhoe field is proceeding at a very fast pace, with five drilling rigs currently active; each rig drills and completes a development well every thirty-five days. The British government is 48 percent owner of BP, which in turn will own over 50 percent of Sohio by 1978. Sohio controls over half of both the Pipeline and the oil leases at Prudhoe. Prudhoe oil, some 9.6 billion barrels of it, is the supposed answer for Project Independence, the federal government's program to develop a "domestic" oil supply, free from control by the policies of foreign nations.

Charlie growled to the bus full of tired workers again, indicating there was an arctic fox outside. It was loping along the roadway sniffing for scraps of brown-bag lunch jettisoned by drivers bored by the lack of comfort or surprise. The billowy white fox, a puffed handful of wool casually surrounding two bituminous eyes as deep as mineshafts, placed his ear to the snow to sound for the scampering of mice and lemmings underneath. It was a bad year for lemmings, they'd all run into the sea only a year or two before. He wandered pointedly, plotting the slight streaks of tone change in the crust, memorizing the intricate network of caverns, reconstructing the mazeways and generating matrices of chance, under the snow, fastidiously learned in order to survive in the Slope's harshness.

Once the bus arrived in camp in the midway dark of winter, its occupants quickly jumped to the camp's arctic entrance double doors, or were immediately rewarded with minor frostbite on all exposed flesh, just in the time it took to grab a suitcase with a bare hand. One man's vinyl bag split when he set it down in the snow for a moment; all of his underwear and gear fell

into the snow and began to blow away. Finally he checked in, got a room, and walked on and on through the corridors of what seemed like Ice Station Zebra, or Little America under the Anarctic ice, launched on some expansive Jules Verne fantasy. Technological fantasy is a genre invented for American readers, concerned with comings and goings in fantastic machines, and contemptuous of life at home or in the inn. Prudhoe Bay has over a dozen sprawling camps, designed with the pure pragmatism and apathy of engineers, who seem indifferent to wonder and beauty. The rubber-matted corridors stretch on involuntarily by the mile on the Slope, a labyrinth of tunnels and storerooms hidden from the rasping snow.

The Ralph M. Parsons Company is the managing contractor and principal engineering firm on the Slope, and runs the show for ARCO. The show itself was impressive, a huge working model of futuristic technological monstrosities scattered all over the area, hundreds of miles of piping, thousands of electric poles carrying power lines, hundred-foot-high prefab modules crammed with unbelievably complicated refinery apparatus floating above the white tundra on steel piles and gravel pads. There was nothing human about the scale or the situation, behemoth cubist structures hovering off in the distance whenever not obscured entirely by the rolling, hanging ice fog. Because of a thermal inversion, warm air generated by machines and buildings and generator plants simply rises a few hundred feet and then sits or settles back to earth, a frozen cloud of exhaust. Virtually every cold day at Prudhoe, it is impossible to see more than a half mile.

Lawrence limped down the rubber-tread hallways to the dining room. His rhythm was set some eighteen years ago in East Texas, when one of a hayrake's dozens of pitchfork fingers plucked too many ligaments from the back of his knee, and left him sprawled out on the prickly, dried straw of a week-old cut hayfield. Lawrence checks the glass-cased fire hoses and nozzles every time he passes by; never says a word, just a daily nod acknowledging their presence again, as if to a neighbor.

Lawrence checked the chill factor, minus eighty-five, and took Gregory, the new timekeeper, off on his rounds of the jobsites on Gregory's first day. They went into the Bannister welding shop, where there were probably twenty-five welders and helpers milling around, hybrid creatures in subterranean smoky quartz-faced metal masks and coarse leather work jackets, a cross of blacksmiths and Grecian sponge divers.

Big Bruce totally engulfed a stool in the cramped foreman's office, crudely partitioned off from the open workshop. He was in charge of this crew of Local 798, the pipeline union from Tulsa, Oklahoma, the only group in the world certified to weld forty-eight-inch pipe. Big Bruce and Lawrence exchanged nods, stoically, deliberately. Then he eyed Gregory, an urbane black from Boston, suspiciously, at great length. They basked in mutual assessment for probably a full minute; Bruce's almond eyes, back to Lawrence's azure ones.

Barren contempt flitted across between the two men's eyes and baked expressions, both that peculiar muddy ochre of most all Mexican pottery. Both were East Texans, and Lawrence worked hard to put that fact behind him, to forget the link treasured by the 798er workers. To them, Lawrence was a sellout to management from their own ranks. East Texans are suspicious of everyone save Okies, whom they simply dislike. It was characteristically ignorant of an oil firm to assign a black urban boy to oversee East Texans, the tough kids from the last piece of scrubby pine forest in the South, just where it turns into prairie. In 1930, a field of 1.8 billion potential was discovered, nurturing a local oil proletariat although the history of emigration elsewhere, to California or the Gulf oil fields or now Alaska, continued. The 798ers have extreme pride in their reputation on the international oil circuit. They consider themselves the Marine Corps of the oil business, and travel, eat, and carouse in groups even in Alaska, a state devoted to the solitary individual. Flowered caps and pointy-toed boots are their trademarks;

hard-fighting, drawn-out stubbornness their standard reply to tense situations. In Tonsina, and at Fort Wainwright near Fairbanks, there had been brutal violence with relaxed Alaskans provoked by the terse Okies.

A strange, repressed minority, for the workers with the best developed collective consciousness were the same East Texans so desperate for an identity, who went to extreme measures to establish one. No one suffers so much as Southerners who are uprooted, or Texans trying to strut their way out of oblivion. Deprivation and affluence are ironically similar in the responses they can provoke, the little-minded meanness and subtle cruelty, the dark indifference to others. The ethic of self-made survival that set them adrift has changed form only slightly amid the wealth of Alaska, into gold nugget watches and more Jim Beam whiskey. The 798ers are at once both the Line's most social subgroup, and its darkest sheep, rooted in a bitter solitude that travels wherever they may go.

Oil is the detritus of ancient forests and seas, and is found today in a web of deserts throughout the world. The peculiar desert ecology has spawned a subculture of oil nomads who wander the steppes and bays plying their craft in vast, stale places passed by most, where people cling with uncommon tenacity to what few ritual and social graces are available. The East Texan vanguard of oil has extended itself to another desert, way into the northern snows, to weld pipe and work its way into the host culture with the penetrating powers of oil.

Alaska is the most egalitarian place in the Union, where women drive bulldozers and only subtle class lines exist. It is currently engaged in a galumphing minuet with the aristocratic side of Texas that runs the oil industry, some curious warp of the American frontier ideal. Men are left free to pound leather in the infinitely open plains, to exercise their lasting illusion of innocence with no boundaries to limit their indulgence. The self-made man stubbornly constructs a fantasy of detachment from the web of life, and imagines his own immaculate conception, operating outside of the laws of natural processes. Texans have no sense of the world as a system, of long-term benefit for the species, and no modesty. Open space exists only to be filled. Anyone who goes around proudly declaring "Yes, I'm from Texas!" deserves whatever happens to him.

Back in the camp, *Guns of the Timberlands* lay open on the bed in Johnny Williams's tiny room; work was over for the day. Johnny had just traded a neo-Nazis-in-global-crime story for this Louis L'Amour ("The World's Bestselling Western Writer"), its glossy cover sporting a painting of cowboy and Winchester, sandstone and cougar. Tall, dignified verging on frail, and dressed as if for club sandwiches out on the patio by the practice putting green, Johnny was from Texas. Johnny was worried about being removed by ARCO from the top spot at Central Compressor Plant, a casualty of ARCO's latest embarrassed investiture of its own personnel in key positions on the Slope. ARCO had been having problems at Prudhoe and was entering a new relationship with Exxon, which gained considerable control over affairs there and began to rearrange ARCO and Parsons personnel almost across the board.

"They're going to shuffle 'em all like checkers anyway, so why worry about it and think you're going to make a career out of it here, Johnny?" Marvin, Johnny's roommate, reached for another Coke, to wet down the V.O. still burning in his throat, and dripped it lavishly all over Johnny's hand-tooled Mexican briefcase, a cocoa collage of sombreros, ponchos, and donkeys, with the rich sheen of executive abuse, polished by Johnny's travels to Arabia, Venezuela, everywhere.

"The sonofabitch is a circus, I tell yaa," Johnny agreed, nodding, "a regular carnival here." His tone was like the quiet consultations of oligarchs mulling over the riots down in the marketplace in some banana republic, the new coup by the brash young colonels or those naive students again. "The temperature's forbidding outside, no white man could live out in that weather, I tell you, we're just a different race from these Native types; God

didn't make us right to live here, just to look after things, to watch over the whole show."

"They're fifteen fucking million over budget now. They got . . ." lots of emphasis . . . "down there . . ." each word injected with authority . . . "a million" each word, every one ". . . and four hundred thousand for 'small tools.' Shit! That's a lot of Phillips screwdrivers! You know what their warehouse down behind Flow One costs? Take a guess, goll ahead, guess . . . ahh hundred and ninety thousand dollars — almost quarter of a million! For a fucking tin shed! And PKS has only got two, three percent complete of Flow One, too, that's it. None of this bullshit twenty-odd percent they talk about." Johnny trailed off into another double V.O. on the rocks; it just kept flowing. He is an aristocrat in the midst of a profession inflated by the ambition of its practitioners, struggling *to build* in every vacant, littered softball lot; in deserts and dusty spaces.

Johnny hoped he would be called to the Parsons home office in Pasadena to "straighten out them fellas down there, shit yah, I'm gonna just tell 'em like it is up here. Ain't nothing else I can do, no other way to save this project, it's such a fucking mess now; I just got to *tell 'em* that! that's it." Johnny looked out the window and sipped from his paper cup, hardly a hint of any supreme inner turmoil. There was nothing to see; the window was entirely frosted over.

"Well, Marvin, let me tell yah. I got a wife that does about all I want, yessir, she's really something, that woman," back to the sunny porches, the condominiums, the Spanish moss and cuisine; away darkness. "Shit, that woman is *beautiful,* Marvin, just beautiful! She's from Indonesia, real open and beautiful over there. Ahh, she takes good care of me, yessirrr, Marvin, why she was *raised* to defer to men and look after them. Shit, ahh go home and all of mah shoes are spit polished and shining in the closet, there's never a one that's out of place, nooooahh. Why, at a meal, you couldn't *force* her to eat afore you do, why she'd just fill up her plate, and pass it all around to the others first, never touch a thing until all them others been served. Ohh, that's a good woman! She sure looks after all my stuff, too. Why one time my boy walks into the closet at home and starts to

go out with my golf clubs, an' my wife just stood in front of that door an' said he couldn't take 'em, that she'd die first, they were *mah* clubs — now that's *some* woman, I tell yah . . ."

Johnny went back to the pile of Houston *Chronicle* classified ad sections, collected during his recent R&R. He complained that it "always takes me a good couple months to adjust to a new climate, get a damned cold every time I do, every fucking time . . .

"And my wife and I, we'll just have to get ourselves to Mexico, yessir, south of the border's what I just decided, babe, too damned many wetbacks demanding higher pay, welfare, they don't want to work, nosirree, not a one of 'em, they skunked across the border at night and you can't *get* one of 'em to work in your house for less than forty dollars a week now, hell I just decided, babe, take my family down to Mexico, that's what I'm gonna do." Johnny looked at the frosted window again, huge crystals, and wished he could see out.

Two nights earlier, two members of the 798 welder's union had launched a grievance procedure down in Bannister shop that led to their violently assaulting the head Parsons man on the Slope, while he slept in his room. One of the men had been fired that day, and went down to see the resident camp manager with the union steward. The manager, half-asleep, let them in. The plaintiff, a small but muscular man still in his rough-out leather sleeveless welding jacket, demanded immediately why he had been fired, and threw a punch. The manager held his own until the steward and a friend jumped in and began choking him on his bed. Eventually, the two staff men billeted next door heard the fight, and barely saved him in time. Security guards roamed the hallways all night; it was only a few days after the last of the recent rash of fires set by an unknown arsonist still at large.

Johnny still stared, to see what he could see. The ice fog was everywhere, blanketing everything; it was dreamy and hard to discern distinct shapes. It was late, but he kept talking about how he was getting old and has a beautiful wife and family now, and "that fucking dream the other night, people beating down the bedroom door and gettin' to me with crowbars, shovels,

they're fuckin' animals those crafts people . . . man, ah got to go. . . . A man could get killed up here." They both slept lightly that night.

"Another shot of cognac, son? Make a man outta yah, Marvin, hair on the chest and all that, especially before breakfast. Yeaah, those South American Spanish people sure know the good life, a trick ahh learned when ahh's building that refinery down in Brazil.

"Guess I'll get mah shirt on and head off to work! The tattoo?? Oh . . . 'the flaming sword of youth' ahh call it. That's a mistake ahh made a long time ago," Johnny confided, drawing out the last few words to carry back decades. "Yessir, that was a mistake made when ah was young and foolish, and regretted ever since. . . . No, not South Pacific but down in New Zealand itself, back in nineteen-forty-two. Ah was a volunteer, went in for a couple of hard years 'cause they needed me. Got this in Auckland, out drinking with the boys one night. . . . And ah'd wished it would go away many a time, many times . . ."

Walter, crisp coyote wariness dressed in a fine white sheepskin coat and lamb's wool hat from the Caucasus, was off to Pasadena again after a two-day consulting stay in Prudhoe. "See that bag? That's Arabic . . ." offered Walter to his driver. With only minimal prompting, he rattled off a list of arid place-names — Band-e Chārak, Yazd, Sheykh Sho'eyb, Ra's-e Meydanī — that obviously represented a fair cross-section of desert caravanserai lined with desperate French Foreign Legion troops, seven days' growth of beard; coastal oil field towns; and a well-irrigated leisure life. "Yes, and the hash comes in those flat paddies," he continued, "real dark, we used to buy 'em for eighty, ninety *rials*. . . . But it was the oozing black opium that made the place special, gooey and thick and you just take off for hours, just close down the shop and rumble on down into dreamland. Yup, me and the boys and the local petroleum types would make a run pretty regular, got those dancing girls, too. Some of the Alaskan contractors up here are pretty hip, don't kid yourself, yooo, those babies are smoking the best stuff up on the Slope. But gawd I-ran is a desolate piss-poor place! Mud huts, stinking water — can't touch the stuff, don't want a damned thing to do with those peasants in the villages, no ya gots to roll up the windows and turn up the air conditioning and forget 'em."

Walter, who had learned the oil business in northeastern Wyoming around Gillette and Casper before joining Parsons in California, wore his extra twenty pounds well, clinched up by a wide leather belt bearing his name and personal brand cut in large letters into the back: *Bar Flying W, WALTER, Bar Flying W.* He adjusted his chromium glasses, which had begun to frostnip his nose in the extreme cold.

"Ever since I gave up drinking it's been different. It gets lonesome here, and it's lonesome back at home in the cabin, too, these days. My wife died back in forty-three and I was going to get married afterward, but that woman, she was Episcopal. So she didn't want to marry a man with a different religion, and it never happen. No, never got married again . . ."

Fred Stickman is an Athapaskan carpenter; an Indian for sixty-nine years, a carpenter for twenty-four. He was well dressed for the cold, in a royal blue snow-go suit that's great for the short trapline he still runs in the village of Nulato, down where the Yukon makes its big bend to the south. His muskrat hat covered a boar-bristle crewcut, and a face distilled from a thousand Alaskan archival photographs of dogmushers, caribou herders, and thieves.

Fred and a Norwegian carpenter from Minnesota were out by Mod 4903. He was putting up canvas side

skirting, and it was easy to spot his pair of beautiful Athapaskan mittens with their traditional bright braided cords about the neck, so they won't be lost. From the darkness of the mod, their beaded beauty in Prudhoe's world of pure function was startling. Each bead acted as sole representative of a different color of the spectrum unknown here, in the perpetual mists of off-white.

"Yud going to write something uup on all this fur the papers? It's a pretty intriguing place and uperation . . ." Olaf inquired.

Fred's taut, withdrawn face rose sharply. "Oh you know me then, eh?" and leveled out into a placid pool of wrinkles. The delight of recognition triggered a sudden spread of idiosyncrasy, a return to himself, the freedom to live in the fullness of his usual world, not just a capsule version tarnished by the boredom and indifference of the Line. He tested Olaf's knowledge of his world, of all the letters he'd written to the editors of two prominent Alaskan papers, a constant flow for a decade.

Fred began talking about his most recent letter to the Fairbanks *News-Miner,* "oh, about people with long hair." He motioned to his helmeted head and gestured to Olaf's beard. "And a lot of other things." Definite arrogance, while Fred struck a stance of notoriety by some stacked siding, obviously a man both well acquainted with and endeared to public attention. Even in Prudhoe! they want to talk to me, Fred thought. But Fred is not a journalist, as his life is his only story.

Fred Stickman is one beautiful, blazing soul locked in a lonely, consuming contra dance with system, law, and logic, running long into the night. A hero of sorts, one who translates his continuous dialogue with the white-man's world of hierarchies, efficiencies and machines into the language of the villagers. Stickman's prose is full of incursions on standard English; his letters are written on any scrap of paper. "You see, them editors are always crossing things out; they don't like it too much, Olaf. But the people in the villages, they always say to me, 'Stickman! We haven't seen anything for a lo-onn-ga time. Why aren't you writing? That's all we read in those newspapers!' So I just write again, haaa, whatever's happened to me. Oh, I'll tell you — that letter writing is from the teachers in the church school; they had these little books about Jane and Mary, and that's as far as I got, oh I guess up to sixth grade. That and reading cardboard packages and newspapers . . ."

"Anyway. I had a good job at Nulato School, but I heard so much about the Pipeline I have to go to see it. You know you have to see it to believe it. It's a big thing. . . . No more oil stove for me. I'll stay on the Slope right by the oil wells. . . . I'm tired of living alone in a dirty old house. . . . I just picked up the *Tundra Times,*" the Alaskan Native newspaper, "to see the 'Heated Labor Hearing.' That's what I've been trying to tell the world. As long as the union is involved in the Pipeline there is not going to be not much Native Hire. That much I know for sure. I've been bucking the union for years. I remember the time Peter Kiewit and Sons wouldn't hire Indians at Galena 1955. They wouldn't hire my son. I've been bucking them for twenty-three years, and now I had to join them to go to work on the Pipeline . . .

"Well, I was raised poor. My mother always wanted to save money on everything, mostly grub. I remember the time we had no more bread out hunting. My dad gave me half a slice of bread then next day half a biscuit. Next day he cut it down to quarter slice and quarter biscuit, etc. That's probably why I'm the same way. And when I see it here on the Pipeline, I have to write about it. As a carpenter for years, especially for the air force, I saved a lot on material, saved a lot on man hours. I didn't believe in coffee breaks. It's just a waste of money. They run a motor on the pickup truck not in use all day long at zero weather. People here don't think nothing of it here on the Pipeline." In Prudhoe, trucks run day and night from September to May. Every nine months the trucks are scrapped, and new ones arrive — once by barge or plane, now by road — to be junked nine months later.

"This is the fourth time that the Superintendent tried to get rid of me . . . but I'm here yet. That's about what's been going on about the Local Hire. Course that's one thing the Pipeline ain't going to go through without the help of Outside people. Everybody's in the camps, even from Europe, South Africa, North, etc.

141

But to me it stinks. I still smell him. I ran away from home before I got in trouble with the Fish and Game. Now I ran into trouble here again. There must be same kind of people that work for the state government. I mean them fellows make a big fuss about the oil spill. To me they can spill all the oil they want, as long as I'm making hundred a day here, with no rent, no grocery, no city tax. I heard they spend a million dollars because they didn't want to tear the bears' den. That bear got hundred different dens around. I know because we used to hunt them. The state government people is nuts. Same way up around the Slope Bluff last spring. They didn't want to disturb the birds' nests. They spend another million's there. Them birds could go somewhere else to nest, that's nature. Who the hell wants birds or bear either. We want the oil to pour though. The hell with the oil spill. As long as we get that two percent royalty. I hope they throw that oil spill out of court. It looks to me like little kids playing, try to beat each other for nothing. . . ." Fred strode back out into the cold and dazzling white light of midday, to bark at the others and drive nails into the brittle wood that frequently splinters and cracks in the bitter temperatures.

One night of blistering cold, Olaf randomly "borrowed" a truck and stole off to Fred's room in another workers' camp some ten miles away. It was very dark. The auxiliary quartzite driving lights on top of the four-wheel drive had little impact on the whipped, rolling ice fog. Drifts and road looked precisely the same in the creeping night of darkest, lightest Prudhoe.

Fred was lying on his unmade bed in a T-shirt. His beautiful Athapaskan fur and moosehide mittens hung from a hook in the faded wall, and the blue snowmobile insulated overalls stood rigidly in a corner, a full suit of armor awaiting the dawn. The union boss knew Fred well, and always arranged for him to live alone. This gave him plenty of time to read the newspapers scattered on the floor and extra bed, and the *True Romance* magazine — "the only one I like . . ." — by the light of a single bare bulb. Fred relaxed and began to talk openly.

"So the other day was fifty-one below zero. I was out working. But we have space heaters here. Not like when I used to trap in a tent every winter, man, that was cold. No time to build a cabin. Also the new Governor should look into how much a week Uncle Sam is stealing out of my checks without asking me — five hundred dollars a week. Believe it or not. I could support at least four wifes with all that money like long time ago. One medicine man had three wifes, but when he got the fourth one, he started to have trouble. . . . That's one man's opinion, but the reason I'm always writing is I don't like to see it happening to the rest of the young generation . . ."

Fred talks easily about his most private worlds, and they begin to glow alive and free. There is something of the chieftain, of the shaman, the man of knowledge and visions, that exudes from him as a master of his element, a wanderer in the woods and the rumpled ravines of the Athapaskan spirit world. "You know," he began again, "I knew you were like me, Olaf, right away I did. I had a dream about that the other night, someone came from away far off to ask me questions and just talk about important stuff on and on. . . . So I recognized you, both of us knew. I was back in my old cabin, it was re-eal dark outside, and then my kin came, a family person, and did some strange noises and said lots of strange things. . . . There were animals around, too, you know, they were talking about me those animals, an old poor man all alone in the cabin, and you know what? My mother came to me, just like the old days, working by the fire and pots on the grub, she said it would be cold soon, so I knew I was going back on the Pipeline, and sure, the union in Fairbanks guy, he called on the radiophone to the village store the next day, so here I am at this Prudhoe Bay. Another time my lead dog was sick, and I had this dream about it, and . . ." Fred talked on and on, an open channel to a raw, crackling psyche; a brilliant force lighting up four torn, featureless walls.

Fred is used to hard, steady work, and has had trouble adopting the very different tactics necessary on a cost-plus job like the Pipeline. There is a skill to lasting on such a job, an ability to always look busy while actually doing nothing at all. Learning to live with the uncer-

tainty, the indecision, the commuting to work every day for an hour each way in an old school bus; all of it takes its toll. Fred hates the bus ride as much as anything; it's enough to send him home, maybe. So in camp, he sometimes plays pool in drafty recreation halls, not caring about winning; he sometimes fills the soiled bedroom floor with crumpled newspapers, unread.

He lies on his bed now, right now, holding both triceps and hugging himself as if the torrid room were really drafty. A coughing, sad and wistful man drones on some more. . . . "But there is a lot of good things here. Good food, good cooks, good baker, good maid service. What I miss here is gambling, and of course the African girls, like Anchorage. They go after you, and beg you, then they rob you also. You can't win. . . . It's a good place for an old bachelor like me, especially when you come off the Slope, with all that easy money. . . . Things won't or can't change too much. Everything is running smooth with the North Slope money . . ."

Flow Station Two is one of two major gathering stations for the ARCO field, where feeder lines from the wells deliver their crude. The oil undergoes preliminary refining to ready it for the Pipeline itself, a few miles south at Pump Station One. Due to a few slight miscalculations, the entire complicated contents of Flow Two were sitting out in the blowing snow and minus-seventy-five weather, rows of skids sporting bent, curling piping and tanks in what appeared to be a junkyard for broken-down steam calliopes. There was not a sound inside the gigantic main room, the size of an airplane hanger, despite the fact that twenty-five workers were supposedly on the job. Snow whipped through the veritable wind tunnel unabated, as the corrugated iron siding at one end had been stripped by the Sheet-metal Workers and the Ironworkers so that the Teamsters could maneuver and load their rigs and the Operators could pull the one-inch steel cable hooked onto the hospital-white unused refinery apparatus and drag the forty- or hundred-ton skids out into the cold as the Laborers swept the area and the Pipefitters bolted plywood discs over the open pipe mouths all around the Electricians and the subcontractor's field engineer and timekeeper as they oversaw the whole show. Three Laborers launched themselves into the scene, lethargically dragging brooms across the snow-swept floor.

Craig and Randy and Mr. Haupt were at first a mite bewildered by the snarls of pipes and dials surrounding Flow Two, like some NASA trial run in the desert for the colonization of Mars. But they had come to realize that the dismantling of Flow Two was a two or three million dollar tragedy in two acts. Flow Two was 90 percent ready for flowing crude when it was scrapped in February of 1976. Mr. Haupt illuminated the irony and infamy of the situation to his two friends. "They had some kind of misinformation about the composition of the crude here and designed Flow Two specifically for that type. Then, a while back, they realized the stuff coming out of the ground was significantly different. So, we gotta tear down the walls, drag all these skids full of gadgetry out into the snow and just throw them away, and then we gotta jackhammer holes in the concrete floor and put thirty-nine more piles in. See how Two is way close to the ground, only three-and-a-half feet or so, compared to Flow One and the other buildings? This was built right after the strike back in about '70 and built wrong — too close, it'll melt the permafrost and sink. They just did it too damn fast without thinking. Then we gotta pour another concrete foundation 'cause this one's too thin to support all the weight, then we build some more space and drag all the new equipment in."

Mr. Haupt tucked his blanched nose into his fur ruff for a moment to warm it. His head was overly large for his body, and featured a somewhat flattened face that was almost Asiatic. Mr. Haupt was an electrician at the site: brick-built, world-wise, with a fine understanding of arctic construction practices gained over twenty-odd years of work in the North, at its most isolated outposts. Mr. Haupt had spent most of the last two decades

frozen-in in construction or maintenance camps, and he knew how the snow blew, how it piled, where it came from. But he was only an electrician and no one listened to his mild suspicions and condemnation of plans that wouldn't work. Mr. Haupt is a stocky and centered arctic proletarian of German design who alternately marched and lumbered about the wastes like a well-disciplined penguin. He also knew about cost-plus contracts, how mistakes don't matter, how it's not worth raising one's voice. Flow Two was a little-known embarrassment to the oil technocrats of Pasadena and Seattle.

The slight change in composition of the heavy, high-sulfur Prudhoe crude had necessitated a complete revamping of the processing system, because of the high degree of specialization in the production sector of the petroleum industry. For the same reason, there was not enough refinery capacity in California for the specific Prudhoe product, as the industry had not made sufficient renovations to the equipment there. The most Alaskan crude that could be handled in California by the projected 1.2-million-barrel-a-day capacity flow of the Pipeline in 1978 is roughly 970,000 barrels daily. The oil is needed in the Midwest and Northeast, but was going to California. The Friends of the Earth had maintained in 1974 that the Pipeline was "the wrong way to deliver oil to the wrong place." The congressional act authorizing the Pipeline in 1973 expressly forbade sending the oil to Japan, the possibility of which would have made a strong case for the alternate Canadian pipeline route down the Mackenzie River to the Midwest. Senator Ted Stevens of Alaska pointed out, two years later, that "Alaskans do not want our oil shipped overseas, but without an adequate pipeline system, that may be the only option." An economist at Standard Oil of California explained at the same time that "An exchange with Japan makes good sense. Exchanges like that are a way of life in the oil business."

The problem was an atrocious lack of planning by the industry, or simply an interest in seeing the oil go to Japan, source of the forty-eight-inch pipe, in a complex, lucrative exchange for Middle Eastern crude earmarked for Japan. Japan and Alaska are intricately interwoven as colonist and colony. Hordes of Japanese tourists — they always travel in large groups, unusual themselves in Alaska — overladen with the complement of Japanese cameras that seems to be issued automatically with Japanese passports, throng the largest airports and the main tourist attraction, McKinley National Park. Japanese entrepreneurs are winning enormous contracts for Alaskan timber, seafood, land, and minerals, and already ship liquefied natural gas to Tokyo from a plant on the Kenai. Mighty, modern Japan is hungry for raw materials, and in a search through the Third World that has taken Japanese managerial expertise to Hawaii, Brazil, Indonesia, the next stop is Alaska. There is terrific irony in this oddest of couples, the small, shrewd, group- and duty-conscious Japanese with the hulking stature and beards of the independent Alaskans; a return to the Asiatic origins of the state's first occupants. Alaska is a colony of the United States, but of the Japanese as well. As its nonrenewable resources, its mineral wealth, are being utilized in new schemes controlled by Outside interests, Alaska is moving into an era of increased technological specialization, in industries that are highly capital intensive and only a very distant cousin of the gold ore rocker and sluice.

"I hope they figured it out better this time," Mr. Haupt remarked. He pulled at the heavy tape on the elbow of his stained, experienced Eddy Bauer Karakoram down parka. "Don't make much difference to me," Mr. Haupt reiterated, "just makes the job go a little longer up here. We could do all the work necessary in a week or so but they got their own ideas about it, be a couple three, four weeks probably 'fore they get it done. We'll just sweep the snow out, take a break to watch it blow back in, and then sweep it out again for four weeks. Get all sweet and ready for the whole fleet of new modules they're bringing up on the barges come August. Yeah! the whole guts for this place, twice the size it is now, is coming by barge from Seattle, through the pack ice. Assuming they *make* it this year, and there's no screw up like last year. Haa! *Still* got all those tugs and barges frozen in the ocean. Hey, what do you think the rent is for all that big marine freighting equipment, eh? Haa! That's a good one! All the oil's going to Japan anyway, it doesn't make much difference to me." Mr. Haupt's eyes twinkled with amusement and his entire body beamed for a moment, the way it always did when humored.

"Craig! Randy! Guess you ought to push those blocks over the side again soon as this damn wind stops blowing. Then sweep the snow out again, soing as we can look busy as bees, case the boss comes by."

"Okay, Commander!" Craig and Randy replied with a snap to attention, broom handles over their shoulders in mock military posture. They were identical twins in dress, both in regulation-issue Alyeska parkas consisting of a lightweight down liner, and a heavy, ironically forest-green Nomex Aramid down-filled outer: chemical- and flame-retardant, water-repellent, lightning-grounded, earthquaker-tolerant, too bulky to allow knavery, and capped with a coyote-fur ruff. The ruff was mandatory in arctic conditions because its long hairs broke the wind around the face to prevent frostbite, and warmed the frigid air that was inhaled. The parkas, liberally lined with reflector tape for night and winter work, available with matching down pants, had become a symbol of Alyeska and the Pipeline, in all their obesity. The parkas swarmed the streets of Fairbanks, although they were only available to Pipeliners, and received knowing judgment from long-time Fairbanksans. At Orientation, lines formed in an army barracks basement at Fort Wainwright — different colored lines on the floor guiding recruits through the maze of corridors all built at bizarre angles, in case an enemy should attack the base — to try on and finance, usually through paycheck deductions, the long list of required arctic gear. It was the facemasks of wool or felt or vinyl, though, that set Alaska apart in winter, the masks that everyone wore in the streets of Fairbanks and the wastes of Prudhoe to protect them from exposure to the wind that cuts through all defenses. Only the Eskimos and a few Indians didn't wear masks in Prudhoe; they only make them at home to show to the whites, the tourists.

"Okay, Commander!" they spoofed again, as Craig yelled, "Pressennnt . . . Brooms!" and they executed the order before being almost knocked over by a blast of ice crystals through the wall. "Jesus! It's eighty-five outside today" — in winter in Alaska, the "minus" is dropped from conversation, and instead a "plus" is added whenever necessary — "and it's usually colder inside the metal shed here. And here we are, sweeping out a whole arctic blizzard every half hour or so. Randall, our mission is to carry on in spite of the odds arrayed against us, and the sheer, unfathomable Catch-22 idiocy of the task, and collect our fat paychecks again the day after tomorrow."

Craig was a Ph.D. candidate and teaching fellow in anthropology at the University of Oregon before "seeing the light" and junking that for the Pipeline. He and Randy were roommates and were both married to women working as Laborers in Prudhoe, who also shared a room. The arrangement allowed the couples to spend all their nights together. Craig and Fern were a Pipeline family: they had met in another camp, worked together, taken some time off to live in Fairbanks, and then both had been dispatched to Prudhoe. When the two of them arrived as a married couple, the Alaskan subcontractor was appalled and immediately called the union hall in Fairbanks for two new Laborers to replace them. The replacements turned out to be Susan and Randy. The women were not at all accepted at first, despite the low status, simple laborer work. In other unions, especially the Teamsters and Operators, the mystique of technology and machines was considered incomprehensible to women and caused initial hard feelings among the men, who had lost one last preserve. After two weeks being protected and written off as a loss by the subcontractor, the firm's boss openly referred to the two women as his "best workers on the job, wouldn't trade them for anything." Because Fern had been in four other Pipeline camps and was clearly married, she was granted deference by the five hundred men. Fern was a mellow gypsy mountain lady with one thick braid of chestnut hair to her waist, who had traveled the continental mountain circuit: Idaho; Telluride and Boulder, Colorado; Vermont; Fairbanks. Now she had settled down in Prudhoe, or some other camp, for a projected five years.

Craig had decided that the academic life was an august fantasy that bore no resemblance to the real world, to what was important in life. He was given to rambling dissertations on the quality of life and technical anthropological analysis of the Pipeline camps and subculture, at dinner or during daily sweepings of Flow Two. But most of the time, he clothed his thoughts in the standard Pipeline sarcasm, the dark humor that chided racial and regional groups, especially Texans.

Fern, always with Susan, swept a different frigid module at another maze of wiring and scientific logic a few miles away. One that housed an enormous computer center that will operate all aspects of the Prudhoe field: pumping the crude, distillation, diversion to Pump Station One on the actual Pipeline, compression and injection of the natural gas back into the oil-bearing formation to maintain the proper pressure, all by remote control. In case of a leak, though, it was the job of the computer in the Valdez Terminal, eight hundred miles south, to recognize the failure and close the appropriate valve. Alyeska admits that some fifty thousand gallons a day could spill from the pipe indefinitely without detection. In winter, the entire Pipeline would freeze solid if the 145-degree crude were to stop flowing for twenty days due to sabotage or repairs. A Soviet pipeline south of the Arctic Circle in Siberia reportedly suffered a break that shut it down for over a year, due to the plugging of the pipe and pumping machinery. If the Pipeline broke in winter, as state Pipeline coordinator Charles A. Champion put it, "you'd have the world's biggest Chapstick."

"The big joke in Fairbanks awhile back was 'If a Bechtel man and an Alyeska man fall from the top of the Polaris Building at the same time, which one would hit the ground and splatter first?' The answer's obvious: 'Who cares?'" Craig adjusted his nutmeg-colored Carhart insulated oversuit to divert the wind from a slender gap between wool scarf and down jacket. There is an awesome memory at work in Alaska, and it misses little. The harshness of Alaska is that the wilds are all eyes, they see every faltered step, the forfeit of each solemn promise. An unbuttoned cuff or ill-fitting glove is sought by the wind and cold, and found.

Filing jointly, Craig and Fern figure they will clear $80,000 a year. Their goal is put aside a quarter of a million dollars from the Pipeline, "as long as they pay this kind of money — we figure there's maybe five years' work left up here — then just retire and raise goats and kids in Oregon," out where Ken Kesey lives. "Life is difficult and dangerous, so we need to be as careful as possible in living it. I can't keep my head in the right place while working at any job but life. There's that Eskimo poem from somewhere that goes: 'A wonderful occupation/ Hunting caribou!/ But all too rarely we/ Excel at it/ So that we stand/ Like a bright flame/ Over the Plain.' Guess that's about where it's at for me, just want to sit back and stroke my blond beard for the rest of my days."

Craig felt that he and his wife were involved in a vision quest out in the tundra, a personal search in the arctic vastness for a life that was correct and meaningful for them. It was something that the Northern Plains Indians had gone through to mark the passage from adolescence to adulthood, when they underwent duress until they saw some sudden, hallucinatory sign of how they should lead their lives. Everyone in camp, everyone in all Alaska now, had a plan or two of how it should be, how things would be different if they saved enough for a plane or forty-seven-foot schooner or investments in condominiums. Amid this wealth of dreams, the most pathetic were the ones with no plans for salvation at all, the ones who couldn't say why they were there. So everyone made plans, just to have them.

"It was a circus up here at first, all the hoopla and big deal money and Gold Rush wild, zany times. But now it's not funny anymore, we've all stopped laughing at the clowns. After a while it all pales, you realize what a lifetime of Big Oil does — the sellouts, the big money, the wild country gone to waste; it all gradually seeps in."

Craig looked down at the snow drifting into Flow Two again from around the sixty-foot-long skids of white refinery. It was almost time to begin sweeping it out into the blistering cold. He laughed, and the cloud of exhaust froze and hovered around his head like a balloon caption for a comic book character. "If greed is the anti-Christ, I sure know where I'm going . . ."

Josh, a black-bearded Teamster from Duluth in his early forties, sat and talked about home with Margery, an older staff assistant for Boatel, the firm with the housing and catering contract for the camps. Josh spoke of his three years on the Slope without too much regret, yet bare of emotion of any kind. He explained that it was about time for his R and R since this was his seventh week, and he'd decided to head home to Duluth for a particularly special two-week leave before returning to Prudhoe. The first time he'd been married was so many years ago he could hardly remember what it felt like, though he did recall that she was a pretty woman who cooked real well. Eight years was all it lasted; he'd been away about six of them. Josh thought his second wife was fine at first, but little things of little consequence soon acquired debilitating stature. For eighteen months he had been a bachelor again.

Josh pulled out his wallet and produced a single, aged photograph of a matronly woman in a mother-of-pearl satin wedding dress. The woman wore her charcoal hair hastily pulled back so that a few strands broke free on their own against the flow, in what seemed otherwise a formal Victorian portrait. Josh explained the special part of the vacation by saying that a good friend had written him about the woman, whom he had never met, and said that they would probably get along fine. They corresponded for several months and had decided to get married upon his return to Duluth the following week. Josh held the photo before him in a somber way for Margery to see the demure bride-to-be, whose eyes were focused at something in her right hand, well off the edge of the picture. He held it up for quite a spell without speaking any word or discoursing with his deep eyes, like a European father after the war, forever searching with a portrait of a lost daughter.

Margery smiled faintly and talked about her own five years at Prudhoe. She had come up when there were only scattered crews doing seismic work and exploratory drilling following the big strike in '68. Quite a few of the Boatel personnel had permanently moved into Prudhoe years ago, and some seldom bothered to take the R and R when it came up, for seasons at a time. She and Josh sat in the hallway near the two telephones that connected the camp's five hundred occupants with the outside world, and watched the line of callers slither by to the tiny plywood booth that allowed some facsimile of privacy, though everyone could hear. Margery went through the catering crew and listed how long each person had been on the Slope: four years, with six months off for a trip to Ohio; three-and-a-half years; seven years; eight years, even before the strike.

"Back then there wasn't all this fancy accommodations, just trailers dragged by snow-cats in a caravan. They wandered all over this place, hundreds of miles, moving 'most every day even in winter, forty- and a hundred-below for months. People got used to it after a while; they get used to anything, you know." The cat trains would load up with supplies and then strike off into the tundra, four or five months at a time without changing crews. They'd start in one direction and go for a hundred miles in a straight line to collect the proper seismic data. Out over the pack ice of Prudhoe Bay, out into the Beaufort Sea, the Arctic Ocean, the shallow continental shelf scoured by constant winds. She talked about the crews out there now, moving fast all winter, every day, grinding across the solitude over near Pet 4, and up near Harrison Bay. They would probably be back in May, when break-up came and the protective snow covering melted and roared off to the sea. But that was another three months off, so surely they were out there right now, in the blackness of a winter's night, a night of winter without end.

Darkest, lightest Prudhoe is one windswept crust of whiteness that reflects all light, all colors thrown upon it. Nothing leaves an impression. Blanched beaches, driftwood, ice floes and cloud banks, a totalitarian blizzard of sameness. It has always been this way, much of every year and aeon, pure explosions of ivory landscape without bounds. But in winter, the sun seldom rises and it sets soon thereafter, and the ivory weathers brown. A clumsy, heavy blackness arrives, it comes right out of the ground.

Capped oil wells, Prudhoe